Acclaim

Life from the Top of the Mind

"I've read this book three times now, and I'm happy to say that my first impressions were extremely accurate: Exceptionally easy to read yet filled with powerful and enlightening concepts and day-to-day living tools. Dr. Crawford has put so much together into a cohesive whole. Thank you!"

> Robert E. Dybala - Licensed Clinical Social Worker & Licensed Professional Counselor

"Dr. Bill Crawford has a rare gift for breaking through interpersonal communication barriers, and his "Life from the Top of the Mind" philosophy is a "must have" for any individual looking to be a more effective leader in their business or personal life. His involvement with our organization has been instrumental in building healthy management and employee relations. He has helped us architect the kind of professional working environment I have always dreamed of. I want to personally thank him for bringing the models and methods in this book to our organization, and for re-energizing our company's focus and direction, and I know that our employees feel the same way."

> Jennifer Cole, MS CCC-SLP President, Cole Healthcare Services, Inc.

"We live in a time of dramatic paradigm shifts that challenge all of us to re-imagine the ways we have tradi-

tionally understood ourselves and our relationships. As we seek to understand the source of chaos, stress and disease in our world, we are led to new insights that have the power to transform our lives. In "Life from the Top of the Mind," Dr. Crawford not only gives us a wealth of new information that can inspire such a transformation, he also gives us the practical tools to make it happen. Bill Crawford has a powerful gift of making complicated material accessible, memorable, and practical in application. If creative transformation is your goal, "Life from the Top of the Mind" can be your road map!"

Charles Gaby, MA, LPC
Director, Center for Creative Transformation

"Dr. Crawford has marvelous insight into the human mind and its power over the body. His approach to dealing with the stresses of everyday life and with difficult people is the best medicine that any doctor could ever hope to prescribe. This book should be required reading at every medical school and for every healthcare administrator in the country!"

Andrew S. Rombakis, M.D., Physician,
Former Surgeon, Emeritus Administrator, and
Regional Consultant for Kaiser Permanente
Northern California Region

"Having worked with Dr. Crawford's philosophy and system, I can attest firsthand to their power and effectiveness. In Life from the Top of the Mind, he gives us a book that uses common language and common sense to both explain how emotions affect decision making, and more importantly, gives us a method for regaining con-

trol of this process in all aspects of life. For those who are interested in the latest cutting-edge thinking with respect to individual and organizational effectiveness, you will find what you are looking for in this book!"

Victor Frazao, President and CEO, Frazao Insurance, Trumbull, Connecticut

"Life From the Top of the Mind is one of those rare books that can change your life! From chapter to chapter, Dr. Crawford boils profound principles into practical steps for addressing daily challenges and living a life of purpose. This book isolates the source of our 'failures' and 'successes,' and helps us reprogram ourselves for happiness and effectiveness. As you dive into Life From the Top of the Mind, be ready to come out the other side transformed from the inside out."

Joe Frodsham, Author of *Make it Work: Navigate Your Career Without Leaving Your Organization*. Former Director of Leadership Development for Whirlpool.

"Genius is the ability to reduce the complicated to the simple" said C.W. Ceran. This book is an excellent example of Dr. Crawford's genius for reducing the complicated process of managing our emotions and accessing our best thinking into an easy to understand, step-by-step system that we can all use to negotiate life's challenges and build effective relationships. I highly recommend Life from the Top of the Mind to any individual and/or organization that wants a fresh perspective and scientifically based system for becoming more effective."

Dr. Jimmy Smith, Organizational Consultant, Owner & CEO of The Retreat At Artesian Lakes

LIFE
FROM THE
TOP OF THE
MIND

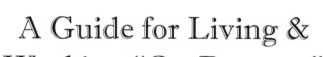

LIFE
FROM THE
TOP OF THE
MIND

A Guide for Living &
Working "On Purpose"

Bill Crawford, Ph.D.

Florence Publishing
Houston, Tx

First Edition: Copyright © 2006 Bill Crawford, Ph.D.

Second Edition: Copyright © 2008 Bill Crawford, Ph.D.

Third Edition: Copyright © 2017 Bill Crawford, Ph.D.

Manufactured in the United States of America
Cover by Steve Butler
Text Graphics: Created by Bill Crawford with additional illustrations by Dover Publications, Inc., Tim Teebeken of Artville, L.L.C., and Georgia Crawford.

Bill Crawford, Ph.D.
Crawford Performance Solutions
Email - DrBill@billcphd.com
Website - www.billcphd.com

Florence Publishing
Houston, Tx

To my wife, Georgia,
and my sons,
Christopher and Nicholas
with all my love.

Life from the Top of the Mind

Acknowledgments

Each time I attempt a project as all-encompassing as writing a book, I am reminded of how much the talents and contributions of others play an integral part in creating the final product. I am grateful for the opportunity to thank these individuals for their support.

Let me begin close to home and start by thanking my wife, Georgia, for her support, patience, and enthusiasm for this project. Not only did she spend many a sleepless night proofing and making changes in the final manuscript, she did this while continuing her multi-generational role as loving mother to our two sons, Christopher and Nicholas, and loving daughter to her mother, Mrs. Socrates Rombakis. I am continually amazed at how having her as a relationship partner has enriched my life and allowed me to do the work that I do from a foundation of love. Further, not only has she been a significant factor in the creation of this foundation, she continues to be an example of the power of love as a resource for recreating a sense of family on a daily basis.

Let me also thank my two sons, Christopher and Nicholas. They continue to be a reminder of the importance of being purposeful in my role as a father so that I am always mindful of responding to life in a way that I would be proud for them to emulate. This book, as well as, everything else I do, is dedicated to Georgia, Christopher, and Nicholas, with all my love.

Next, I would like to thank one of my closest friends, Steve Butler, for his work on the cover of this and all of my previous books, as well as my website. His expertise in graphic design has greatly enhanced the look of the book, as his friendship continues to enhance my life. His consistent genuineness, humor, creativity, and quality of character make him a joy to work with.

In addition to all of these wonderful people, I want to be sure and thank my mother-in-law, Efthemia Rombakis, and my father-in-law, the late Dr. Socrates Rombakis. I can't imagine getting this far in my career and being able to write a book such as this without their love and support.

And finally, I would like to thank my mother and father, Florence and Burton Crawford. Even though they passed away almost 26 years ago, I am touched daily by their warmth, love, and philosophy of life. Their commitment to creating a loving home for me, as well as helping others through the programs of A.A. and Alanon has given me a foundation on which to build a life and a life's work. In many ways, they live on in every word of this book.

Contents

Part I

Part II

Introduction

As books go, I'm proud to say that this is my fourth of seven. My first two on *stress* and *dealing with difficult people,* were written in conjunction with the two PBS specials that I had the pleasure to film in Houston, and later make available to the nationwide PBS network. The third was a book on *parenting* entitled, "How to Get Kids to do What You Want!" A popular title (as you might imagine), this book was written to (a) provide parents with a guide to interacting with their children in such a way that results in their kids paying more attention and following their instructions better, and (b) show parents how to teach the qualities and characteristics they want their children to have when they become adults.

As a result of my recent work with students in the performing arts and college students, in general, I have also written "Freeing The Artistic Mind," "Parenting The Young Artist," and "College From The Top Of The Mind."

I say all of this to give you some sense of how this book fits into my work as a psychologist, and how it is both similar, and yet very different from my previous works. The similarity is that the models I use in all of my books have remained intact, and I have also incorporated some of the examples I used in previous works to illustrate how to apply the material to real life. However, what makes this book different, and hopefully more valuable is that this is the first time I have attempted to combine all that I know into a comprehensive guide, which is now being updated.

The necessity for this combination became apparent in my seminars and coaching sessions as the challenges that people identified became increasingly complex. When I was doing a presentation on *stress,* one of the principle triggers participants always seemed to identify would be the difficult people in their lives. However, because I had only enough time for the material on stress, all I could do was allude to the other book. Similarly, when I was doing a presentation on *dealing with difficult people, conflict resolution,* and *successful communication,* it became clear that until the participants were able to shift from their reactive, "stressful" way of perceiving the situation and/or person, they would have little success in applying the material on interpersonal effectiveness. Thus, once again, I would find myself alluding to the material in the "other book," but not having time to go into it. With my coaching clients, I was more successful at blending the two, however, there was still the challenge of drawing from two sources and attempting to combine the material to deal with the situation in a more holistic manner.

What became increasingly clear is that individuals and organizations needed a comprehensive system that addressed the complexity of life, and gave them all of the information they needed to succeed. As a result, I have written this book, "Life from the Top of the Mind," in which I bring everything I have learned from my perspective as a psychologist, corporate trainer, executive coach, husband, father, self-employed entrepreneur, and planetary resident for over sixty five years.

In terms of how the book is organized, all of the material and models presented are developmental in nature, meaning that each new concept not only addresses a specific block to success, and also builds on what has already been presented, and further, lays a foundation for what's to come. In order to illustrate how all of the models fit together and support you in becoming more influential in your life and the lives of others, some repetition was necessary. Hopefully you will experience this as reinforcing versus redundant, however, I have tried to err on the side of more information versus less, especially where core concepts are concerned.

Part One describes why the book is necessary, or how problematic situations can trigger certain reactions which create an increasingly debilitating cycle that blocks our ability to succeed. Once this process has been explained, I go on to offer a powerful solution that can be applied immediately.

Part Two builds on these concepts, and presents a series of additional models designed to make the change permanent. Both Part One and Two are about how to deal with problematic situations such as deadlines, traffic, bureaucracy, change, etc. Part Three is devoted to applying all that has been presented to dealing with difficult people, and/or becoming more influential in your interactions with others. Part Four will tie everything together, and give you some suggestions on what to do next in order to become skilled at bringing this "Top of the Mind" perspective to life.

My sincere wish is that you will find this book valuable, and that as a result of reading and working with the models presented, you are able to become more influential in your life and the lives of others. Or, put another way, that you will come to experience the power and promise of living "Life from the Top of the Mind."

Part I

CHAPTER I

The Problem

At the age of 47, George has recently become the CEO of a Fortune 500 investment firm. He works between 60 and 80 hours a week, but seems never to have enough time to accomplish everything on his list, the most important item being how to cut the spiraling IT(information technology) costs that are threatening the survival of his firm. He loves his family, but rarely has time for them, and in general, seems to be running from crisis to crisis, putting out fires and feeling increasingly overwhelmed by life. Unfortunately, this stress is affecting not only his individual productivity, but also how he interacts with his family and his executive team.

Deborah is a 35 year old mother, wife, and

senior account executive for a major investment firm. Having had her first child at the age of 31, there is a part of her that is wanting another, however, she too feels overwhelmed by all of the demands in her life, and thus wonders how she could take on caring for yet another child. It's hard to really know how many hours Deborah works, because she sees herself as having at least two jobs, and goes from one to the other, wondering when she will ever have any time for herself. Unfortunately, this stress is spilling over into her personal life in the form of arguments with her husband, as well as her aging parents who seem to be looking to her more and more for comfort and reassurance, while at the same time rejecting her advice on issues such as long-term care. Plus, her boss, the recently appointed CEO, is becoming increasingly hard to deal with due to his tendency to try to micro-manage everything and everyone around him.

Sean is a 32 year old IT systems expert for a major Fortune 500 investment firm. Sean is becoming increasingly stressed by the fear that his job will be outsourced soon. His wife is employed as a school teacher, and while they seem to be able to get by with their combined incomes, the idea of surviving on just her salary alone is frightening. He is considering looking for another job, but his friends who are also IT professionals say that everyone is trying to cut IT costs, and thus he feels hopeless, trapped, and confused.

What all of these people have in common is that none of them are living life from the "top of the mind." While all of their problems and reactions are understandable, the result is that they become increasingly overwhelmed, angry, confused, and frustrated. Unfortunately, this only makes their problems seem worse, which then triggers another round of stress, frustration, and anxiety, and they become caught in a cycle, or downward spiral that I call "The Cycle of Stress/Frustration."

The Cycle of Stress/Frustration

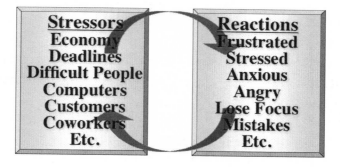

Stressors	Reactions
Economy	Frustrated
Deadlines	Stressed
Difficult People	Anxious
Computers	Angry
Customers	Lose Focus
Coworkers	Mistakes
Etc.	Etc.

Sound familiar? Are there aspects of your life or those around you that are triggering certain reactions and throwing you and/or your people into your own Cycle of Stress? If so, then you have come to the right place, for my purpose in writing this book is to give you a clear understanding of why this seems to be so prevalent, and more importantly, what can be done. In other words, a step-by-step guide to bringing your best to life, even (and maybe especially) in the most difficult of situations.

Before we go any further, I want to emphasize that this is not just another book on "stress management." I'm not going to suggest that taking a deep breath and chanting, "Don't worry, be happy" is the solution to your dilemma. It has been my experience that most people are tired of simplistic answers to life's complex problems. Thus, I will not insult you by telling you what you already know, or that "you've had the answer all along." In fact, I believe that it is just this tendency to try to solve our problems using incomplete information that has resulted in an increase in our stress and frustration. Or, as Albert Einstein says:

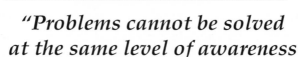

"Problems cannot be solved at the same level of awareness that created them."
Albert Einstein

This means that if we don't have a good understanding (sufficient level of awareness) of what stress and frustration really are, as well as what is creating the cycle, our attempt to address what isn't working won't work. In other words, when we see the triggers, or problematic situations, in our lives as the cause of the problem, we naturally try to change the cause. Unfortunately, because so many of the negative aspects of our lives are not under our direct control (traffic, difficult people, deadlines, etc.) the result is that we feel more, stressed, frustrated, angry, overwhelmed, etc., and the infamous cycle is created and maintained.

Now, just to be clear, I'm not one of those people in the field of psychology that says you have no right to feel this way, or even that you are wrong for feeling angry or frustrated. I just want you to ask yourself one question . . . *How's it working for you? !!!*

I ask this question because most people would say, "IT'S NOT!," meaning that they don't want to go around feeling stressed, angry, frustrated, overwhelmed, or stressed. And, couldn't we easily add "resentful" to the list of reactions? Don't most people resent having to deal with all of these problems all of the time? If so, there is a great quote about "resentment" that might serve us well in our plan to regain control.

"Resentment is like taking poison and waiting for the other person to die!"
Malachy McCourt

I find this quote valuable because it succinctly captures what is going on here. We are feeling understandably resentful of the negative people and / or situations that seem to be causing our problems. Unfortunately, resentment, stress, and anxiety not only doesn't help, they actually make the original problem seem worse, which traps us in a reactive cycle.

I remember a time when I was caught in one of these cycles of resentment and stress. It began innocently enough. I was just sitting in an airport waiting to catch a plane to my next speaking engagement. I was thinking about where I was about to go and what I wanted to say when an announcement came over the speaker system stating that my flight had been canceled. This was years before I had perfected my current method of handling such events, and thus I started to became stressed and worried about what I was going to do. Then I noticed that there were very few people waiting to catch this flight, and I began to wonder if they had canceled the flight because there were not enough passengers to make the trip profitable. Now, in addition to feeling stressed and worried, I became angry and resentful, and I was just about to give those airline people a piece of my mind when . . . "mother nature" called. Of course, as we all know, this is a call that cannot be ignored, and so, oblivious to pretty much everyone and everything around me, I stormed off to the bathroom rehearsing what I was going to say to the people at the airline counter.

As it turns out, the bathroom was empty, and

so I picked a stall, sat down, and was continuing to practice my tirade when . . . someone in a pair of high heels walked in! One would think that this would bring me back to reality with a distinct crash, however, I was so caught up in being "right," I just assumed that everyone else was wrong, and therefore she must have wandered into the wrong bathroom. I didn't want to embarrass her (for after all, it wasn't her fault that the flight was canceled) and so I was trying to think of a polite way to let her know of her mistake when . . . another person wearing women's shoes walked in! Of course, at that moment I realized that I WAS IN THE WRONG BATHROOM!!! Further, if I said something now, it would have looked like I had been hiding in there all along.

As you might imagine, all thoughts and emotions of the canceled flight disappeared and were replaced by worries around my current predicament. I remembered that no one was in the bathroom when I first came in, and thus decided that if I just covered my eyes and didn't make a sound, they would eventually leave and I could escape. Well, about that time a plane must have landed because the place filled up, and I knew that sooner or later someone was going to notice my shoes or just want the stall, and thus the "wait them out" solution was no longer viable. So, mustering all of my courage, I said "Excuse me" and the place got really quiet. Next, I said, "I am not a pervert, this was a mistake, and if everyone will just cover up, I will leave." I then proceeded to exit the bathroom, hand over my eyes, attempting to be as inconspicuous as possible, but having very little success.

How could this happen? Well, clearly I was so frustrated and stressed about the canceled flight that I didn't pay attention to whether the figure on the door of the bathroom was wearing pants or a skirt (not to mention failing to read the sign!) In addition, I was so worried about the original mistake that I compounded it by trying to avoid taking responsibility for my error in judgment.

While hopefully you will never find yourself in this situation, I think it's fair to say that the process of reacting to our triggers with more stress is a familiar experience for most of us, and further, the ensuing cycle is something we would all like to avoid. If so, then I suggest that we draw upon the wisdom of Dr. Einstein, and raise our awareness of what is truly happening in these situations.

CHAPTER 2

The Natural Law of Cycles

The first thing that we need to understand is that there is a natural law operating here, and because we are not aware of this law, we may be using it against ourselves. I call it the "Natural Law of Cycles," which basically states that all of life presents itself as a cycle of cause and effect. In terms of our thoughts and emotions, most people see "the cause" as what happens to us and, of course, when the cause is positive, there is no problem. However, when the cause is negative (the stressor, difficult person, deadline, etc.), then *we* become "the effect," and therein lies the problem.

We Become the Effect!

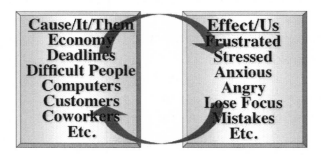

Cause/It/Them	Effect/Us
Economy	Frustrated
Deadlines	Stressed
Difficult People	Anxious
Computers	Angry
Customers	Lose Focus
Coworkers	Mistakes
Etc.	Etc.

When this is the case, there are three ways to change:

1. Change the cause: On some level, this is what most people attempt first, meaning that when they feel angry, frustrated, or stressed, most people try to fix the problem by changing what they believe made them upset and, if this is possible, I think it's a great idea. In other words, if you can influence your environment in such a way that results in your feeling better, then by all means give it your best shot. However, most people find that there are many aspects of life that either resist their efforts to change them, or are just beyond their control. When this is the case, attempting to change the cause only "causes" more stress.

2. Change the effect: The second option involving the natural law of cycles is more powerful, however, it is certainly a road less traveled, because most people don't even think it's possible. It describes dealing with the cycle of cause and effect by changing the effect. This involves changing how difficult situations and people affect us by choosing how we want to respond. Most "self-help" books advocate this approach, and while it is certainly a wonderful skill to have, it is also limited in that no matter how accomplished we become, we are still the effect. This is why I advocate an even more rare and in some ways more radical approach I call "becoming the cause."

3. Become the cause: As mentioned, this third option is even more unorthodox than the first two, and thus it is even more rare. However, I believe that this is the most powerful way to harness the natural law of cycles and deal with the cycle of stress/frustration. In short, rather than advising you to spend your energies trying to change the cause (especially when it is not within our control) or even change the effect, I am suggesting that we flip the cycle and become "the cause," which is what this book is all about.

CHAPTER 3

Changing Stress from the Problem to the Solution

In order to adopt this more powerful perspective (becoming the cause), we must also raise our awareness of the true nature of the problem. In other words, in addition to the Natural Law of Cycles, another aspect of the problem that we need to understand more fully is what "stress" (frustration, anxiety, confusion, etc.) really is, and how we can become more influential with respect to this aspect of our lives.

Interestingly enough, our lack of understanding around this issue doesn't stem from a lack of exposure. You can't turn around without seeing a new book or magazine article about the subject of stress. However, as promised, I am not going to rehash this information or tell you what you already know. In fact, unlike most people who talk about stress, I'm going to suggest that stress isn't even the problem, but actually part of the solution! A quote that I use in my presentations which speaks to this perspective states that:

"Stress is a signal that something needs to change . . . Suffering is when we don't make the change."

I like this way of looking at the subject because it defines stress not as the problem, but rather as a valuable signal that when ignored can lead to the real problem... suffering. For example, imagine you are moving your hand closer and closer to a hot stove. (Kids, don't try this at home!) You will begin to feel "stress" in the form of heat and pain. THAT'S THE GOOD NEWS! If you didn't feel this signal, you would destroy your hand. In this case, "stress" is a valuable signal, and when seen as such, can become part of the solution.

Another good example are the warning lights on the dashboard of a car. Let's assume that we are driving down the road, and one of these warning lights become illuminated. If we dealt with that light the way most of us deal with stress (i.e., saw it as the problem), we might become annoyed and want to reach over, break it out, and keep on driving thinking, "There, now everything is fine." Of course, we don't do this because the little red light isn't the problem, it's part of the solution! It lets us know that something needs our attention. By the way, have you noticed how much more attention we pay to the warning lights on our dashboard versus the warning signals from our body?

Bottom line, stress isn't what we think it is. It isn't what someone or something does to us. ("Stupid people really stress me out," or "Deadlines just drive me crazy") nor is it our failure to cope ("What's wrong with me? "Why do I let all of this get to me?")

What we call "stress" is really just a series of chemical reactions in our brain and body!

I am putting extra emphasis on this statement for two reasons. One, this concept is the foundation for much of the material we will discuss from this point on, and two, this is a unique and relatively new take on the problem. In fact, in the not too distant past, if you wanted to find out how stressed someone was, you would give them a test. This would consist of a list of life experiences (such as death of a loved one, divorce, job loss, a major move, etc.) and each experience would be assigned a weight or number.

The idea was that if enough bad things were happening to you in life, your number would be high, and you would be described as suffering from "stress."

The problem was that not everyone with high numbers described themselves as stressed, while many people who didn't have scores in the problematic range reported being "very stressed." What researchers came to realize is that there had to be other factors operating here, and they began to explore what happens chemically in our brain and body during these experiences. They discovered that there are three major chemicals associated with the experience of being "stressed." These are adrenaline, noradrenaline, and cortisol. Of the three, cortisol is the most important.

In fact, measuring how much cortisol is in one's blood stream is now one way to determine how "stressed" someone is. Of course, this isn't to say that these chemicals are all bad. In fact, if we look at the relationship between stress and productivity, we find that when there is zero stress in our lives, there is zero productivity. . .

It's called SLEEP!!!!!! The fact is that we are not very productive when we are sleeping! Plus, when we are sleeping, there is very little adrenaline, noradrenaline, and cortisol in our body. In fact, guess what chemicals wake us up in the morning? You guessed it, adrenaline, noradrenaline, and cortisol.

So, for a while, as our stress goes up in the form of these chemicals, our productivity goes up as well. In other words, we are more productive three hours after we wake up than we are three minutes after we wake up, and that's because we have these chemicals going throughout our body.

However, as most of us have experienced, as our stress continues to go up, at some point our productivity goes down, and eventually we crash and burn.

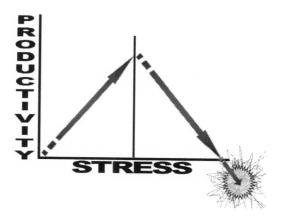

Therefore, following Dr. Einstein's suggestion that the more awareness we bring to a situation, the more successful we will be, I want to help you become aware of when you first feel pushed over the top and begin that all too familiar downward spiral. Then, because stress is just a series of chemical reactions in your body, I want to show you how to use stress as a valuable signal, and actually CHANGE THE CHEMICAL MAKEUP OF YOUR BODY so that you can bring yourself back into your zone of productivity.

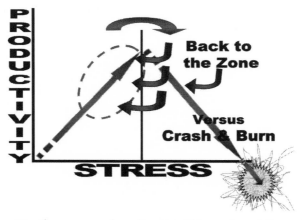

By the way, when I am talking about "productivity" here, I'm not just referring to being productive at work. I'm talking about bringing our best to any aspect of life. Plus, I'm not here to tell you where you "should" be with respect to your productivity. You can bring yourself back at a high level, medium level, or low level. That is up to you. I just want to show you how you can be more influential in this process, versus be controlled by the negative aspects of life.

Okay, now we know about the Natural Law of

Cycles, and the fact that what we have been calling "stress" is actually a series of chemical changes in our body. In order to be able to become more influential in this process, we must also understand how all of this works in our brains (which will also shed more light on just what I mean by "Life from the Top of the Mind.")

Most people have heard that our brains are divided into three parts: the brainstem, the limbic system, and the neocortex.

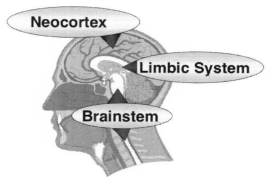

The brainstem (the lower part of the brain) is where our fight-or-flight responses are located, and is also the part of the brain that regulates our breathing, heart rate, blood pressure, and muscle tension.

The middle of our brain is called the limbic system, and this is where our memories and emotions are triggered. What most people don't know, however, is that this part of the brain also acts as a gatekeeper. Or, in today's terminology, it acts as a scanner, a processor, and a router. It scans incoming data, processes it or interprets it, and then either routes it down to the brainstem, or up to the upper 80% of our brain, the neocortex, where we have access to our interpersonal skills, problem-solving skills, clarity, confidence, creativity, etc.

In other words, data comes in from our five senses, and it is first scanned by the limbic system. If the limbic system determines that there is no problem (for example, we are sitting, reading a book), then the data is sent up to the neocortex, the brainstem works in the background regulating our breathing, and all is well. However, if the limbic system senses any problem, anything, or anyone it doesn't like, anything or anyone that it has identified as stressful in the past (i.e., the "stressors" in the cycle of stress), then it sends the information immediately down to the brainstem... **bypassing the neocortex!**

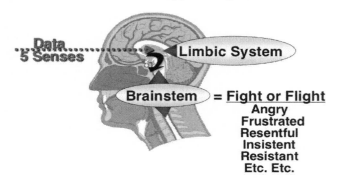

Of course, at this point, the brainstem can only respond in two ways: fight or flight, and so to prepare for this response, this lower part of the brain triggers the release of adrenaline, noradrenaline, and cortisol, which results in an increase of our heart rate, muscle tension, blood pressure, etc. In the latest brain research, this is called "downshifting" because it happens so fast, and again for our purposes, what is important is how this process **bypasses the most intelligent, purposeful part of our brain (the neocortex)!**

Now, to be clear, I'm not saying that this is always a bad thing. In fact, in a true fight-or-flight situation, this is exactly what you want to happen. For example, imagine you are walking down the street and someone jumps out from the bushes. You certainly wouldn't want to have to stand there and think about the situation or your response . . . "Hmmmm, someone just jumped out from the bushes . . . wonder what I should do?" No, in this sort of situation, an immediate fight-or-flight reaction is clearly what is called for, and the good news is that evolution has set us up well for this reaction. Thousands of years of surviving saber-toothed tigers and other dangers has given us a brain and nervous system that reacts to perceived threats in a very specific way.

The bad news, of course, is that few (if any) of the triggers / problems we encounter on a daily basis (deadlines, difficult people, meetings, etc.) are truly fight-or-flight situations. Quite the opposite, they require our best problem-solving skills, interpersonal skills, and creativity in order for us to be successful.

Unfortunately, due to the limbic system hijacking the data and sending it down to our brainstem (in his book, *Emotional Intelligence*, Daniel Goleman, Ph.D., calls this process "neural hijacking"), we are now coming from the lower 20% our brain and producing chemicals that raise our heart rate, blood pressure, muscle tension, etc., and limit our response to fight-or-flight. Of course, when I say "fight-or-flight," I don't mean simply the tendency to either attack something or run away from it. The "fight" reaction can manifest as becoming defensive, argumentative, or rigid in one's position, while the "flight" can show up as depression, withdrawal and/or avoidance.

Further, when we try to deal with the perceived triggers from this limited perspective (hypertensive, stressed, frustrated), we are often less than successful which, of course, has us feeling even more powerless, frustrated, and stressed. The limbic system interprets this additional frustration as even more negative data, and dutifully sends it right back down to the brainstem.

This, of course, triggers the production of even more adrenaline, noradrenaline, and cortisol, which results in a further increase in blood pressure, heart rate, and muscle tension, and the cycle of stress becomes our experience of life.

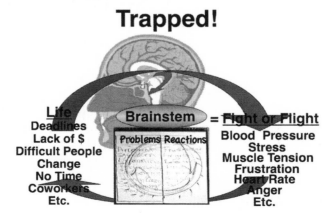

Trapped!

Life
Deadlines
Lack of $
Difficult People
Change
No Time
Coworkers
Etc.

Brainstem

Problems Reactions

= Fight or Flight
Blood Pressure
Stress
Muscle Tension
Frustration
Heart Rate
Anger
Etc.

As you can see, the problem is that we are becoming trapped in the lower part of our brain which cannot solve the problem. In fact,

90% of our frustration, stress, and anxiety is coming from the lower 20% of our brain!

I call this part of the brain our "undermind" because not only is it physically under the rest of our brain, it's also where we feel undermined by the world around us. I also call it the "moat mentality" because this is where many people feel attacked and start focusing all of their energy on defending themselves, their job, data, reputation, etc., by building moats or circling the wagons.

Whatever you call it, what's clear is that this lower part of the brain is no place to live. It doesn't work for George, the CEO, who is afraid of losing his company. It doesn't work for Deborah, the account executive, who is afraid of losing her chance to have a second child. It doesn't work for Sean who is afraid of losing his job, and I'll bet it doesn't work for you!

Therefore, rather than just showing you how to "manage stress" (i.e., keep it down to a manageable level), I am going to give you a model that will allow you to change the chemical makeup of your body, and shift from the world of the undermind (brainstem) to more of a "Top of the Mind" (neocortex) perspective.

I'm then going to give you another model

that will help you stay in this clear, confident, and creative mindset so that you can bring your best to life, and experience the power and promise of living "Life from the Top of the Mind."

For those of you who would like to quantify the degree to which you may be using your brain-stem to deal with life, you can take the "Top of the Mind" Inventory located in the appendix.

CHAPTER 4

Regaining Control

I f, after taking the "Top of the Mind Inventory,™" you discover that you are finding yourself coming from your brainstem more than you would like (or if you just want to be more in control of which part of your brain is in control), the good news is that changing the chemical makeup of your body and shifting from the brainstem to the neocortex isn't as daunting a task as it may sound. In fact, smokers do this all the time. Don't worry, I'm not going to recommend that you take up smoking in order to regain control of your life.

However, I do think it's interesting to note

that every time I ask a smoker or former smoker the question, "Does or did smoking help you deal with stress?" they almost always answer "Yes!" When I ask seminar participants why this is, many say that it must have something to do with the chemicals that are being inhaled. However, nicotine, the principle chemical that is being ingested by smokers, is a stimulant! By all rights, those who use cigarettes should say that they are stimulated by the act of smoking, however most say that lighting up actually calms them down.

What could be happening here that is so powerful it overrides the effect of a chemical stimulant? First, smokers seem to be responding to a signal. They may be working on a particularly stressful project or deadline, and something clicks in their brain that says, "Man, I need a cigarette!" Next, they stop whatever they are doing and go out to the dumpster (because that's the only place we will let them smoke anymore) and begin their ritual. For example, many smokers will do the same thing each time, i.e. tap their pack, light up, and inhale deeply. They will then hold that breath for a moment or two, and let it out in a slow long breath.

In fact, this may be one of the principle reasons smokers say that smoking helps them deal with stress . . . it may be the only time in their life that they take a deep breath! Now, for us nonsmokers, it means we never take a deep breath! We just go around breathing short and shallow breaths until we become really stressed and stop breathing altogether (which, by the way, has been proven to be very hazardous to one's health).

So, what can we glean from this example if our goal is to regain control, change the chemical makeup of our body, and shift our thinking to the top of the mind? First, the smokers are responding to a signal in such a way that a change in behavior (going to have a smoke) becomes more important than anything else. Remember when I said that stress can be seen not as the problem, but a valuable signal that something needs to change? Remember when I suggested that we become aware of when we first feel "pushed over the top," and begin that downward spiral? What if we were to raise our awareness of what stress feels like so that at the first sign of frustration, annoyance, resentment, etc. we could stop and focus all of our attention on regaining control?

Then we could do what the smokers do, i.e., take a deep breath! You see, whenever we are feeling out of control, there is always one thing that we can control and that is our breathing. That's why if you have ever done any stress management, meditation, or yoga, you were probably told to "take a deep breath" when stressed.

The problem with this advice was the implication that this is all it takes to deal with the frustration, anger, and/or anxiety associated with a negative event, and we all know that just isn't true.

In fact, if all we do is breathe deeply when stressed, we will just hyperventilate sooner or later because this doesn't solve the problem. Therefore, I am not going to suggest that this is where we should stop. However, I am going to suggest that this is where we should start, and here's why: Remember, when I labeled the three parts of the brain and described what function each part controlled?

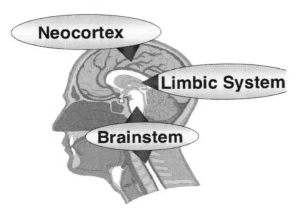

As mentioned earlier, the part that normally controls our breathing is the brainstem. However, when we decide to take a deep breath, the part of the brain that is making that decision is the neocortex! This means that the "Top of the Mind," or upper 80% of our brain where we have access to our problem-solving skills, interpersonal skills, creativity, knowledge, etc., has actually taken over a function normally assigned to the brainstem, and thus has literally regained control!

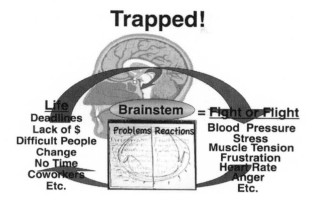

Trapped!

Life	Brainstem	= Fight or Flight
Deadlines		Blood Pressure
Lack of $	Problems Reactions	Stress
Difficult People		Muscle Tension
Change		Frustration
No Time		Heart Rate
Coworkers		Anger
Etc.		Etc.

The key here is to do this slow enough and deep enough to be effective. To ensure that this happens, I encourage you to use what I call the 4-4-4 method. This means that you inhale for a count of four, hold it for a count of four, and exhale for a count of four.

As children, many of us heard our parents tell us to count to ten when we were upset before saying anything, and that was good advice. What they probably didn't know was that *the only part of the brain that can count is the neocortex.* Therefore, when we breathe deeply and use the 4-4-4 method as well, we are ensuring that this powerful upper 80% of the brain is in the process of regaining control, and we are in the process of becoming more influential in our experience of life.

Another advantage of coming from the neocortex is that this upper 80% of the brain triggers the production of different chemicals. Rather than experiencing the effects of adrenaline and cortisol, you are now beginning to trigger the production of serotonin and endorphins, the chemicals that help us think clearer and feel better. That's the good news. The bad news is that this only deals with one aspect of the "cycle of stress," so let's move on to ensure that the system you are learning is comprehensive in its ability to both deal with the problem, and sustain a solution.

CHAPTER 5

Dealing with Tension

The second characteristic of being stuck in the "undermind" is *muscle tension*. This is due to the chemicals released when "stressed" and again, is generally controlled by the brainstem. This tension is usually experienced as a tightness around the neck and shoulders, however, it can also manifest as tension all over the body and/or headaches.

In my seminars, I help participants understand the effect of this aspect of the problem by having them tense up all of the muscles in their body and then trying to accomplish some task. What becomes clear is that regardless of the simplicity of the task (even if it is only mental), the tension will interfere with their ability to be successful. Plus, this exercise explains one of the reasons why so many people feel so exhausted today. Even though most of the work we are doing is not physical in nature, many people report feeling fatigued at some point in their day. This is because our brainstem is producing chemicals that tense our muscles, and we are constantly fighting this muscle tension while trying to accomplish everything on our list.

Fortunately, there is a word that will deal very nicely with this tension and that word is "relax." Unfortunately, there is a problem with this word. Have you ever gone up to someone who was clearly stressed and said, "Listen! If you would just calm down and relax..."? Would it be fair to say that they generally don't say, "Gee, never thought of that. What a wonderful idea." No. The most common response to this suggestion is defensiveness.

"Calm down?!? Don't tell me to calm down!@#$%&*#@!!"

In other words, they will most likely start defending their right to be stressed! Why? Because in our culture, most people believe that if you aren't stressed, you must not have enough to do or you just don't care about your job, project, family, etc.

This is why when asked, "How are you doing?" most people will not respond with, "Happy and relaxed, thank you" even if this is true! In other words, even if they do feel happy and relaxed, they are reluctant to tell anyone out of fear that it will be misinterpreted as meaning they don't care, or that they are not taking their job seriously. In fact, when asked, "How are you doing?" most people will start complaining about all the "stuff" that they have to do, and how they will never get it all done, which is meant to convey that they have plenty to do and that they do take their responsibilities seriously.

Bottom line, because our culture sees "relaxing" as giving up or giving in, or at the very least what one can do only after one has checked off everything on their list, we see it as a problem instead of part of the solution. In fact, our culture has a name for people who relax before they have checked off everything on their list...we call them lazy slackers!

As you can see, there are several problems with this perspective: (A) Muscle tension is a natural, chemical response to a perceived threat and emanates from the brainstem. (B) Unless the situation calls for a fight-or-flight response, this muscle tension will only interfere with our ability to be successful, and even produce fatigue and exhaustion. (C) What is needed (relaxing to diminish the muscle tension) is seen as a character flaw. Therefore, to be successful we must redefine the word, "relax," so that it becomes part of the solution and supports our neocortex ("Top of the Mind") in regaining control.

When I think of the word "relax," it reminds me not of giving up or giving in, but of another term I learned in childhood. I grew up in a small town in east Texas with "older" parents. In fact, my mother and father had been married twenty-five years before I was born, and I was their only child!. My mom went to the doctor when she was 45 years old and said, "Doc, I'm sick," and he replied, "No, you're pregnant," which, I'm sure brought about at least as much surprise (and maybe even stress) as it did joy.

Suffice it to say I wasn't a planned child. However, there was a positive aspect in my being born so late in their lives. You see, my father was an alcoholic and had been drinking for 22 years of their marriage. He stopped drinking three years before I was born, which means instead of being born and raised in the home of an active alcoholic, I was brought up in the home of a recovering alcoholic, and trust me, there is a huge difference.

The way my Dad stayed sober was through the program of Alcoholics Anonymous (AA) which means that we went to A LOT of AA meetings! In fact, we went to at least three to five AA meetings a week. However, rather than seeing this as strange or abnormal, I just thought this is what everyone did!

As I grew and learned how to read, I began examining the sayings posted on the walls of these gatherings and, as you might imagine, there were quite a few ("One day at a time," "Let go and let God," etc.) that, even at a young age, I found meaningful. My favorite, however, was the "Serenity Prayer" which of course says, "God grant me the serenity to accept the things I cannot change, the courage to change the things I can, and the wisdom to know the difference."

This has become a very popular prayer. However, I wonder how many of us have ever looked closely at how it's put together, and what it's really saying. It's not the "get it all done" prayer or the "make everyone be the way I want" prayer. It isn't even a plea for serenity, or a promise that serenity will be the reward for accepting what we can't change and/or changing what we can. The Serenity Prayer is actually a formula for success!

For example, let's look at the first line: God grant me the serenity to (so that I might first) accept the things I cannot change. Think for a moment . . . how much of your stress, frustration, resentment, etc., would be gone if you could accept what you cannot change? To what degree would this ability diminish the negative effects of traffic, deadlines, difficult people, etc. and support your success? For most of us, this ability to "accept" would make a significant difference in the amount of stress and/or frustration that we experience on a daily basis.

Now, just to be clear, I'm not one of those people who say: "You can't change the world, you can only change yourself." I believe in being as influential as possible in all aspects of our lives. I think we all can agree, however, that when we are frustrated, angry, frazzled, and stressed, our influence is diminished because, for one reason, people don't view overly emotional people as having high credibility. They tend to write them off as "out of control" or "not knowing what they are saying."

Plus, we now know that when we are feeling these negative emotions, we are trapped in the lower 20% of our brain and limited to either fight-or-flight. Basically, we don't have access to the sort of interpersonal skills, problem-solving skills, clarity, confidence, and creativity that allow us to impact the world around us.

This is where the Serenity Prayer can help. For example, serenity and acceptance (the first two things that are asked for in the Serenity Prayer) allow us to do two things. First, serenity, being a neocortex perspective, ensures that we are coming from the top of our mind. From this upper 80%, we can make more purposeful decisions about how and where we focus our energy. Once we have accepted the things we can't change (which allows us to avoid wasting our energy on people and problems over which we have no control), we can set about "changing what we can," which we all know will often take courage. Put it all together and you get a formula for success.

First, we create a moment of serenity which allows us to accept what we can't change. Then, because we are now coming from our neocortex, we can summon the courage to change the things we can, which for the moment is the chemical makeup of our body, and also which part of our brain is engaged in solving the problem. Once we have accomplished this, we will be in a much better position to bring this top of the mind perspective to the situation and see if there is indeed some way we can be influential.

Given that we have just made serenity a very important component in our ability to access the "top of our mind," let me ask you a question. On average, about how many minutes a day would you say you spend creating serenity in your life ? If you're like most of us, the answer would be zero! Most of us wake up in the morning to an alarm clock, and then commence pushing the snooze button repeatedly until we absolutely "have to" get out of bed. This means we are already late, and so we rush through the routine of getting ready (and if we have kids, getting them ready). While doing this, we are often worrying about what problems our being late are going to cause. We then get in traffic, which we resent and fight in a vain attempt to make up for the time we overslept, and when we get to the office (or wherever) we rush to get as much done in as little time as possible.

When lunchtime comes, we take thirty minutes for lunch, struggling to eat as much as we can in the smallest amount of time. Then, we are back doing whatever we consider to be our job, again with the goal being to get as much done in as little time as possible. Finally, it's time to go home, and so we get back in traffic, resenting the fact that we are "forced" to spend so much time in our car. Eventually, we get home, and if we are parents, the "second shift" starts, where we are trying to get our kids to eat more of the "right stuff" (or at all), and then we are trying to get them to go to bed so we can finally have some time to ourselves. They don't want to go to bed, however, so we get angry and say and do all the things our parents did to us (that we swore we would never do to our kids) until they either become exhausted, or we become intimidating enough to make them go to bed. Then, finally, we are sitting on the couch, it's about 10:30 p.m. and we are watching re-runs of sitcoms, thinking that at last, we have found serenity. No! That's not serenity, that's exhaustion!

This is why serenity is the first thing that is asked for in the prayer. In order for us to succeed, *serenity* must be a precursor to acceptance, courage, and change...not just what we get at the end of the day or after everything has been checked off of our list. In the same vein, the word "relax" isn't just an admonishment for being tense, but instead incorporates the concepts of serenity, acceptance, courage and change into one very powerful command. Plus, when paired with the purposeful behavior of taking a series of deep breaths (i.e. saying the word "relax" on each exhale) this further establishes the neocortex as "who's in charge." Why? Because, when we are stressed, worried, frustrated, etc., the brainstem is engaged, and in addition to increasing our heart rate and blood pressure, also increases our muscle tension.

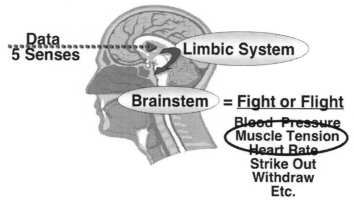

Therefore, when the neocortex gives the command to "relax" on the end of each breath, it once again is taking control and overriding one of the functions normally controlled by the brainstem.

The key here is to do this combination of behaviors (breathing in deeply and saying the word "relax" on the exhale) in such a way and enough times to be effective. In other words, just inhaling quickly and barking "relax" when you exhale will not produce the effect you want. While small, our brainstem is very powerful, and is used to being in charge when problems arise. Therefore, it will take a very concerted effort to go against what seems to be "natural" (i.e. running the problem over and over in our mind and justifying our anger and frustration) and choose serenity over righteous indignation.

If, however, you have determined that coming from the top of your mind is important to you, taking three to five slow, deep breaths using the 4-4-4 method, and saying the word "relax" on the exhale will deal very nicely with the first two physical aspects of stress. Let's move on to what I call the psychological aspects of stress, frustration, and anxiety.

CHAPTER 6

The Psychological Aspects of a Top of the Mind Perspective

A s mentioned, breathing and relaxing, while helpful, will not completely solve the problem, because in addition to the physical aspects of stress, there are very powerful psychological factors at work here as well. One of these is what has been called "mind chatter," negative self-talk, or what I call "brainstem questions."

For example, think of the last time you dealt with a stressful, and/or problematic situation. Do you remember the sort of questions that were running through your mind? Wasn't it something like, "What is wrong with these people?" or "What is wrong with me, why can't I get it together?" or "Why do I always hit the worst traffic?" or something similar?

While common, questions such as these are problematic because of the effect they have on our brain. For example, in certain ways, our brain works like a computer. If you ask a computer a question (i.e. type it in and hit "send" or "enter"), it will go searching its data banks for the answer. It doesn't stop to determine whether this is a good question or bad, helpful or not helpful. It simply attempts to answer the question that is asked. Plus, the answer must be in the particular database that is being searched in order for the computer to find it. In many ways, our brain is the same way.

For example, when we become stressed, frustrated, etc., and start asking questions, such as, "What's wrong with me?" or "What is wrong with these people?" our brain thinks we want the answer! Further, because these questions are about the problem, our mind goes searching its problem-focused database (the brainstem) and probably comes up with responses like, "Well, you're just not good enough." or "These people are just stupid idiots!" and ,of course, this doesn't help.

You see, we are using our computer-like mind to search the wrong database, or asking ourselves brainstem questions to which we really don't want the answer, or at best, questions that don't offer any solution. In fact, they produce chemical reactions that actually make the situation seem even worse and trap us in the lower 20% of our brain.

Given that what we want is to shift from the

brainstem to the neocortex, I suggest that we continue to ensure that this upper part of our brain is in
charge by asking "neocortex questions," or questions
that shift our focus from the problem to the solution,
and allow our brain to search the data located in the
"top of our mind." In other words, we take three
to five deep breaths saying the word "relax" on the
exhale, and then we ask a question to which we do
want the answer. I'm going to give you a lot of these
neocortex questions later in the book, however , a
simple one could be, "How would I rather be feeling?"

Interestingly enough, when I ask this question
to participants in my seminars, the first response is
often a blank stare. This is in stark contrast to their
enthusiastic participation when asked to describe
the problems in their lives and how these problems
made them feel. However, when I ask the question,
"How would you rather be feeling?" most people,
at first, have no reply.

The reason behind this lack of response is
simple. When we are focused on the problem and/
or the pain of the problem, we are coming from the
lower 20% of our brain, and thus cannot imagine
(much less answer questions about) a solution. This
is why there are two steps prior to asking, "How
would I rather be feeling?" The deep breathing and
saying the word "relax" on the exhale are designed
to allow our neocortex to regain control so that we
can begin asking questions about the solution versus

continuing to fume about the problem.

Once I have given participants in my seminars time to shift to their neocortex, most eventually do come up with answers to the "How would I rather be feeling?" question. Interestingly enough, the first answers are often the antithesis of the problem. In other words, if they were originally stressed, they now want to feel calm or serene. While I certainly have no problem with people choosing to feel calm over feeling stressed, I want to be careful not to imply that this is the only choice. For example, rather than feeling calm, some people would like to feel confident, powerful, happy, or excited.

The good news is that in this model of change, you can choose any response you like, which means that you will not be forced to become calm when you would rather be excited, or serene when you want to feel confident and powerful. The important thing is that you allow the "top of your mind" to choose how you want to feel so that you have a neocortex-generated goal versus a brainstem-generated response.

CHAPTER 7

Dealing with Worry

O f course, as important as this third step is in the process of shifting from the brainstem to the neocortex, just asking ourselves about how we would rather be feeling doesn't accomplish this shift. The reason that this question is necessary but not sufficient to create change is due to the fact that when most of us are stressed, frustrated, etc., what we are actually doing is worrying about some problematic person or situation.

We are worried that something either has gone wrong, is going wrong, or will go wrong, and are most likely spending much of our time running this problematic scenario over and over in our mind. In fact, we may even see our worry as a necessary part of solving the problem, i.e., if we didn't worry, we wouldn't be thinking about the problem at all.

This tendency to see worry as a sign of caring, importance, or at the very least, a necessary aspect of successful problem-solving is a big factor in many people's lives. It's almost as if we judge the degree to which someone is involved or engaged in a situation by how worried they are about it. Lots of worry (stress, consternation, etc.) is interpreted to mean that a person is appropriately engaged in solving the problem, and/or is working at capacity, while little to no worry means that they don't care, or don't have enough to do. Further, we tend to see people who aren't worried as unprepared. For example, when you meet someone who isn't worried, don't you get a little worried about them... almost as if it's dangerous not to be worried?

It's my belief that this mindset originates in childhood. Just think... when you were a little kid and you were about to go out and play, what did your mom almost always say to you? Was "Be careful" one of her admonitions, and didn't this really mean "Watch out for bad things happening? Plus, our parents even told us what we should be worried about, such as playing in the street, men with candy, big dogs, etc. In other words, the message was that if we worried sufficiently about the bad things that could happen to us, somehow we would be safe from them, or put another way . . . worry keeps us safe.

Just to be clear, I am not suggesting that we

shouldn't tell our kids to be careful. However, if we look at the word "careful," what it really means is "full of care." My guess is that when as children we heard our mom say "Be careful," we did not interpret this to mean "be full of care for yourself and others." No, we heard this as "watch out (or beware of) bad things happening to you."

The problem, of course, is that unless we are in a true fight-or-flight situation, worry doesn't keep us safe, but rather it sends data to the lower 20% of our brain and limits our ability to respond. Further, all of this change in brain function and triggering of stress-related chemicals happens whether the situation we are worried about is happening at the moment or not!

In my seminars, I demonstrate this phenomenon by asking the participants to imagine holding a lemon. I suggest that they feel the weight of the lemon, and see the bumpy, yellow rind of the lemon in their hand. Then, I ask them to imagine cutting the lemon in half, feel the lemon juice running down their hand, see the shiny yellow pulp on the inside of the fruit, squeeze the lemon and watch the juice squirt out, and even begin to smell the lemon juice. Finally, I ask them to imagine actually taking a big bite out of their lemon, and feel the juice squirt out in their mouths!

As you might imagine, at this point most people are wrinkling up their faces, swallowing excess saliva, and basically reacting as if they had actually bitten into a real lemon! Of course, the lemon was only in their imagination. They knew that they weren't biting into a real lemon, but their brain and body reacted as if they were! In other words, the production of excess saliva and wrinkling of the facial muscles (which were actually reflective of chemical changes in their mouths) was a reaction to an imagined stimuli that they knew didn't exist! They had just changed the chemical makeup of their body, not by what they held in their hand, but what they held in their imagination!

How does this apply to dealing with our worries about life? Well, when we find ourselves worrying about something, how often is that particular situation actually happening at that particular moment? Is it fair to say not very often? This reminds me of a cartoon noticed on a tombstone on which was written the phrase, "Ninety percent of what killed me NEVER HAPPENED!!!!!!

What this demonstrates is that the body responds chemically to any image we hold in our mind, whether it is actually happening or not!

Of course, the problem here is that not only are we producing chemicals which throw our body into a heightened state of tension and stress, but also the fact that what we are worried about isn't actually happening (which means we can't do anything about it at the moment) and this only adds to the feeling of powerlessness and frustration.

In my seminars, I often bring up another example of the power of our mind to create chemicals in our body by asking the participants how many have ever had a sexual fantasy? Then, before anyone can answer, and while most are chuckling at the prospect, I point out that during the fantasy, they knew whatever they were imagining wasn't really happening . . . but their body thought it was! Meaning that again, our body changes chemically to any image we hold in our mind.

How does all of this relate to "worry"? Well, when we are worrying, aren't we almost always creating an image of what we are worrying about? Don't we see the problematic person or situation very clearly and in great detail, and further, don't we spend a lot of energy running this image over and over in our mind? If so, now we know why this rarely helps us solve the problem, because, rather than helping us access the most creative and skilled parts of our brain, the problematic image is seen by the limbic system as a threat, which results in our brainstem being activated and our options limited to fight-or-flight.

Further, as we have discussed, the brainstem produces adrenaline, noradrenaline, and cortisol in response to this image, and thus elevates our heart rate, blood pressure, and muscle tension.

For those of you who are interested in how this reaction effects your health, here's how all of this works. When cortisol is released by the brainstem, it rushes throughout our body, shutting down our immune system (as well as other nonessential functions), shutting down the production of protein, and increasing the production of glucose.

If we are not in a fight-or-flight situation where we either need the extra energy provided by the glucose, or are engaged in the sort of physical activity that would burn it off, it (the glucose) just sits in our system and turns into sugar. This is why if you have ever worried for any length of time, you might find yourself becoming nervous and fidgety, almost as if you have eaten too many candy bars.

It's also why many people have a hard time losing weight when they are stressed and upset for extended periods of time. They are constantly producing extra glucose/sugar from the ongoing production of cortisol, and this just turns into fat. (For more information on how to become more influential in the process of losing weight and keeping it off, see my ebook entitled, "How to Eat Anything You Want, Anytime You Want, & Never Gain Weight!)

Further, our immune system is based upon white blood cells, and the building block of white blood cells is protein. Therefore, when cortisol is constantly rushing throughout our body shutting down our production of protein, we have less protein available to build white blood cells, we have less white blood cells available to strengthen our immune system. . .AND WE GET SICK! Now, remember, this part of the book is about the negative effects of worry, so I don't want you to WORRY about this! I just want you to know that we have the power to influence the chemical makeup of our body by the images we hold in our mind.

How can we use this phenomenon to our advantage? Well, we can see stress/frustration as a valuable signal and at the first sign of this reaction, we can have our neocortex regain control by taking three to five deep breaths using the word "relax" on the exhale. We can then further solidify our neocortex as the dominant part of our brain by asking "neocortex" questions, or questions to which we DO want the answer, as well as questions that lead us away from the problem and toward a solution, such as, "How would I rather be feeling?" Next, we can use the fact that our body will respond chemically to any image we hold in our mind to imagine feeling what we want to feel versus worrying about the problem.

The most powerful way to practice this imagining is to first think of a time in your past when you were feeling how you want to feel now. For example, if you want to feel calm, just think of a time when you have felt calm in the past. The same applies to confident, in control, serene, or however you want to feel at the moment. Unfortunately, some people have difficulty with this step because they try to imagine a time when they felt calm, confident, in control, etc., in a situation that is similar to the one they see as the problem. In my seminars, it is common for participants to say, "Well, sure, I'd like to feel calm in traffic, BUT I'VE NEVER FELT CALM IN TRAFFIC, so I have nothing to draw from."

Fortunately, there is a simple answer to this dilemma. You see, it's not important, necessary, nor even expected that you will have a memory of feeling the way you want to feel in the current situation. All you have to do is remember a time in the past when you felt calm, confident, in control, or however you want to feel now. Remember, the body will respond chemically to any image we hold in our mind, so just remembering a time in the past when you felt how you want to feel now is a great first step.

It is important, however, for this image to be as vivid as possible. For example, remember how I described biting into the lemon in detail? What you may have noticed is that I included many of our five senses in the description (feel the weight and texture of the lemon in your hand, see the shiny, yellow pulp, smell the pungent odor of the lemon, and finally taste the bitter juice by biting into the lemon). Similarly, you can use all of your five senses in remembering a time in the past when you were feeling how you want to feel now. . . where were you, what sounds did you hear, what was the temperature of the air, what aromas did you smell, if you reached out and touched anything in your image, what would it feel like (texture)? Bottom line, the more you engage all of your senses, and the more detail you employ in creating this image, the more successful you will be in effecting the chemical makeup of your body, which generally means producing endorphins versus adrenaline and cortisol.

This is not to say that you should just imagine yourself relaxing on a beach somewhere. Unlike other methods of dealing with problems and/or becoming more successful, "Life from the Top of the Mind" doesn't just try to give you a mental escape from the challenges of everyday life. Or, put another way, this isn't about helping you escape to your "happy place." This methodology is about how to bring a certain mindset to life, and by so doing, effect (a) the chemical makeup of your body, (b) the part of your brain that is engaged, and (c) ultimately, your ability to influence the quality of your life. Therefore, the idea is to create an image that is as close to real life as possible so that it isn't the setting that is creating the effect.

Once you have created this detailed multi-sensory image of the past (feeling the way you want to feel now), the next step is to bring the feelings of calm, confident, in control (or however you want to feel) into the present. Again, this is done with the most powerful part of your brain, as well as the part over which you have total control...your imagination. In other words, first you create a detailed image of a time in the past when you were feeling how you want to feel now, and then ask yourself, "If I were able to bring these feelings into this present situation, how would I change? That is, if I were able to bring this sense of calm, confidence, and a feeling of being in control into dealing with deadlines (for example), what would be different? How would my mannerisms change? How would my tone of voice change?

Of course, since this is all done in your mind, you have complete control of the images you create and thus, you can answer your own question and create an image of you being however you want to be in any situation (work or home, dealing with deadlines, difficult people, kids, etc.) Again, the more detailed and multisensory the image, the more it will effect the chemical makeup of your brain and body, so don't hold back.

Finally, since we will most likely be dealing with many of these scenarios (deadlines, difficult people, work, kids, etc.) in the future, rather than worrying about them (which actually is practicing engaging the brainstem and feeling bad), we can ask ourselves how we would like to deal with these situations in the future. We then create a detailed multisensory image of how we would like to respond, and this act of imagination becomes almost as powerful as a behavioral rehearsal, which means that rather than spending our time applying our mind to worrying about the problem, we have trained it on a vision of the solution that we control.

Okay, let's put all of this together and see what we have accomplished so far:

1. We have identified that certain triggers/situations/types of people, etc. have been interpreted by our limbic system in such a way that it triggered certain emotional and behavioral reactions such as stress, frustration, anxiety, etc., which make the original situation seem worse. This triggers another reaction, and the cycle of stress/frustration is born and fed.

2. We have also identified how this external cycle is replicated by an internal cycle. Our limbic system sends information about the problem down to the brainstem (bypassing our neocortex), which in turn releases chemicals that increase our heart rate, blood pressure, and muscle tension. This, of course, limits our ability to respond to either fight-or-flight. We then attempt to solve the problem, but because we are now tense, hyperactive, stressed, frustrated, anxious, and/or confused, we are less than effective, and thus become even more frustrated, tense, etc. The limbic system interprets this increase in negative emotion and decreased effectiveness as more negative data, and thus sends it right back down to

the brainstem. As a result of all of this, we become trapped in the lower 20% of our brain.

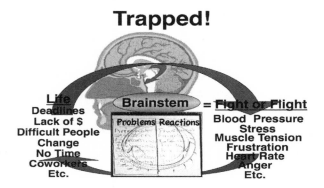

3. We have learned that in order to break this cycle and bring our best to life, we must change the chemical makeup of our body and allow the "top of our mind" (our neocortex) to regain control.

4. One of the most effective ways of doing this is to have the neocortex take over one or more functions normally driven by our brainstem. Therefore, taking three to five slow, deep breaths while saying the word "relax" on the exhale not only establishes the top of our mind as the most influential/dominant part of our brain, it also deals nicely with the muscle tension normally associated with stress.

5. Having accomplished this, we now can ask more purposeful, neocortex questions (such as, "How would I rather be feeling") which directs our neocortex to identify what we want (in terms of how we want to feel) versus focusing on others, or the

pain of the problem.

6. Finally, we can actually change the chemical makeup of our body and thus change how we feel by imagining feeling/being the way we identified in the last step (calm, confident, in control, etc.). We do this by utilizing the phenomenon that any image we hold in our mind produces a corresponding chemical change in our body, whether it is actually happening or not! Therefore, as we imagine being this way (what is our body language like, our tone of voice like, how do we talk to others when we are calm, confident, and in control?) we ensure that our neocortex is in control and producing serotonin and endorphins rather than the adrenaline, noradrenaline, and cortisol associated with worry and/or frustration.

We are now ready to complete the first model by noticing or acknowledging the changes we have just produced (more calm, confident, in control, etc.). This is important because it allows us to take note of and appreciate what we have accomplished, which again is a neocortex activity.

One of the characteristics of an overly stressed, nonproductive mind set is that there is often little attention paid to achievements. Many hours are spent worrying about how problems from the past will negatively effect the future (which we now know only enhances the potential of this happening), but little if any thought is given to what has gone or is going well. The fact that we have just allowed the top of our mind to regain control, relaxed our muscles so that we aren't fighting ourselves, shifted our thinking from the problem to the solution, and changed the chemical makeup of our body is quite remarkable. In order to take full advantage of these efforts, we must now "Notice" these changes and give ourselves credit for the transformation. Plus, this last step, "Notice the change" makes the model spell BRAIN (Breathe, Relax, Ask, Imagine, Notice the change).

When I create models, I almost always try to make them spell something for several reasons. One, it makes the model (in this case, the BRAIN model) easier to remember and practice. Two, we are talking about changing how our "BRAIN" processes information, and signals other parts of our body to produce chemicals, and therefore the spelling supports the goal.

Of course, every model comes with questions and concerns, and this one is no exception. One of the concerns that participants voice is their fear that working through the model will take too long. They think they don't have time to breathe, relax, ask how they would rather be feeling, imagine feeling this way in the past, present, and future, and then notice the changes. In fact, after hearing me present this model, I'm sure some people are thinking, "I don't have time to do this! If I had time to go through this model, I WOULDN'T BE STRESSED IN THE FIRST

PLACE!!#%&*@%!!

While I can certainly understand this concern, I think we may want to look a little deeper at this resistance if living life from the "top of the mind" is truly our goal. For example, I suggest that the reason we think we don't have time to go through a model such as this is that we are not making our peace of mind and/or our ability to deal with stress/life a priority, and I believe that this is a mistake. In fact, I think our peace of mind/ability to come from the most productive part of our brain should be important. . . at least as important as, well . . . diarrhea!

Yes. . .diarrhea! Well, just think, when you have diarrhea, it becomes pretty important, doesn't it? Don't we stop everything we are doing to take care of it? We stop driving on the freeway, talking on the phone, everything! Notice, when people have diarrhea, they never say, "I don't have time to deal with this now," or "I'll just deal with this later." Plus, our culture even supports the importance of diarrhea in our lives. For example, when you are talking with someone and say something like, "Excuse me but I have to run to the bathroom!" have you noticed that no one ever says, "Oh no, you stay right here!" No! Diarrhea has such universal importance that it is acknowledged as an excuse to stop anything! In fact, it's in the building code! You can't build a building without so many little rooms that if people have diarrhea, they can go there! How many "peace of mind" rooms do you see?

That's why I suggest that we make our peace of mind, our ability to access the most productive, intelligent part of our brain and bring our best to life at least as important as diarrhea. If we would stop whatever we are doing for diarrhea, we should be willing to stop when we find ourselves trapped in the brainstem as well. This where the phrase, "Stress is a signal that something needs to change" comes from, as well as the concept that "stress isn't the problem, but a very important part of the solution." Just as most of us respond very purposefully to the signal of diarrhea, we can begin to use stress as a valuable signal as well.

For example, when we first begin noticing the signals of stress (frustration, tension, anxiety, etc.), we can stop, excuse ourselves, and go to the restroom (or any other locale that offers us the opportunity to take a few minutes to regain control.) We can then begin to access our neocortex by taking three to five deep breaths, and saying the word "relax" on the exhale. Next, we can begin to ask more purposeful questions that have our brain searching the data in the "top of our mind" versus our brainstem for the solution (such as "How would I rather be feeling?") Further, because any image we hold in our mind creates a corresponding chemical reaction in our body, we can then use the most powerful part of our mind (our imagination) to change the chemical makeup of our brain and body by imagining feeling this way in the past, present, and future. Finally, after noticing or acknowledging how we are now more calm, confident, and in control, we can go back into the meeting, conversation, or whatever environment we were in knowing that we have shifted from our brainstem to our neocortex, and are now responding from the top of our mind.

So, now I have given you a process (the BRAIN Model) for changing the chemical makeup of your body and shifting from your brainstem up into the top of your mind. As you might imagine, many people are excited to learn that stress is really just data being sent to the wrong part of our brain, which means it's not only something they can control, but that it can even be used as a valuable signal. The only problem with this process is that it is new, and thus has yet to become a habit. Therefore, if you would like to become skilled at influencing the chemical makeup of your body and how your brain processes information, then I encourage you to look for opportunities to practice this powerful model.

In fact, I encourage you to put this model to the test by using it in as many negative situations as possible. This should give you very good information as to how this behavioral model supports your ability to regain control and establish the upper 80% of your brain as the dominant influence of your thoughts and emotions.

Of course, most people want more. They not only want to know how to change or shift when stressed, they are interested in information that allows them to sustain this "Top of the Mind" perspective so that they don't keep falling back into the brainstem and the cycle of stress over and over again.   That's coming up in Part Two.

Part II

CHAPTER 8

What _Doesn't_ Change

The first part of this book has been about what to change and how to change. When feeling frustrated, stressed, anxious, confused, etc., you now know how to use these feelings as valuable signals that a change is needed. You have become more aware of what is happening chemically in your body and brain, and how to use the BRAIN model to change. The second part of this book is about how to maintain this new "top of the mind" perspective, regardless of the situation, or, put another way, how to live life based upon what _doesn't_ change.

"There's a thread you follow.
It goes among things that change,
but <u>it doesn't change</u>.
People wonder about what you are
pursuing.
You have to explain about the thread,
but it is harder for others to see.
<u>While you hold it, you can't get lost.</u>
Tragedies happen, people get hurt
or die, and you grow old and die.
Nothing you do can stop time's
unfolding.
<u>You don't ever let go of the thread!"</u>

William Stafford

As you might imagine, this can be a much more involved process, and thus, I will introduce several models to support you in this new way of life. However, because so many people have told me that they find the BRAIN model to be tremendously valuable, I have also woven this behavioral process into this new material with the goal of tying every-thing together and helping you succeed in living life from the "Top of the Mind."

In order to accomplish this goal of sustaining a "Top of the Mind" perspective, we must first have a good idea of what this new way of being looks like. I call it "**C³**" which stands for *Clarity, Confidence,* and *Creativity.* I use these words not only because they represent universal aspects of success which emanate from our neocortex, but also because as we examine the problem in terms of the cycle of stress/frustration, we can see that there is very little clarity, confidence, and creativity contained in the cycle.

CLARITY
CONFIDENCE
CREATIVITY

In some ways, we have been using the model from the beginning of this book. If you remember, we began with a quote from Albert Einstein that said "Problems cannot be solved at the same level of awareness that created them." In other words, trying to solve our problems by just becoming less stressed, or worse, trying to change the negative aspects of life so that we are no longer anxious will never work. Instead, we must raise our awareness (clarity) about what is really happening to cause the problem before we can access our confidence and creativity to break the cycle of stress, and sustain true success and happiness.

Basically, this is what we did in Part One. We became clear about what really creates and sustains this cycle (the way our brain works and the chemicals it produces), and we learned how to shift to the more productive part of our brain and change the chemical makeup of our body.

However, in order to move beyond simply breaking the cycle to the point where we can actually access our confidence and creativity on a regular basis, we must become clear about other things as well. Therefore, I am going to continue to frame the material in Part Two in terms of "clarity," and demonstrate how an increase in awareness leads to a similar increase in confidence and creativity.

CHAPTER 9

Clarity About the Power of Purpose

The first step in the process is becoming clear about our purpose. I say this because I don't believe that when we are caught in the cycle of stress we are responding to the negative aspects of life "on purpose." In other words, few if any of us are deliberately becoming frustrated, stressed, anxious, or confused when faced with challenges such as deadlines, difficult people, etc. That doesn't mean we don't have a purpose. It just means that it hasn't been chosen deliberately. In fact, you may have heard some people, when coming from the lower 20% of the brain, say something like, "If I can just get through the day (or the meeting, or the project)," meaning that their goal is to survive some particular situation. While understandable, the problem with this perspective is that "survival" is a brainstem experience that triggers fight-or-flight chemicals, and traps us in the lower 20% of our brain.

Therefore, I am going to suggest that we ask a more purposeful, neocortex question... or a question that can only be answered by the upper 80% of the brain. For example, what if, when caught in the cycle of stress, or anytime for that matter, we were to ask ourselves, "What is my *highest* purpose here?"

The good news is that we would no longer be focusing on merely surviving. The bad news is that this question, while "neocortex" in nature, may be a little too vague or general to help us move in a specific direction. In other words, when we say "highest purpose," what are we talking about... feeding the hungry, housing the homeless?

There is a quote I have found that may help us answer the question, "what is my highest purpose?" in a way that is more clear and concrete. It says:

"Every thought, emotion, and behavior is a statement about who we are, and who we are becoming."

Adapted from Neale Donald Walsch

Which leads to another question: When we are caught in the cycle of stress, reacting to life with anxiety, frustration, anger, etc...

"Are we defining who we are or are we being defined by the difficult people and situations we encounter?

You see, when we say "_____makes me_____" or traffic makes me anxious, or difficult people make me angry, or my family drives me crazy... what we are *really* saying is that the negative situations and the negative people in our lives have *the power to define us, or control us!*

If we don't want these problematic situations to have this sort of power in our lives, we must take on that power ourselves. That means that in order to sustain this "Top of the Mind" perspective, we must make defining who we are the most important thing in our life our highest purpose!

Now, when I suggest this in my seminars, I often hear people say, "Well, my kids are the most important thing." or, "My family, relationship, business are the most important thing in my life." and I understand. I have a family, I have kids, I have a business, and I know how important these things can be. Therefore, to be clear, I'm not saying that they shouldn't be important. I'm just saying that they shouldn't be the *most* important thing. Why?

Because there will be times when things happen with our kids, our family, our business that will not be in our control, and if these are the most important thing in our life, that will trigger, stress, frustration and anxiety. Therefore, I suggest that:

You never make the most important thing in your life something that is beyond your control!

Remember, this is about clarity, confidence, and creativity. Which means we must start with clarity, and we must be clear about three things:

1. *The purpose of the negative situations we encounter.* How have they affected our lives in the past? Is this working for us? Are we using them, or are they using (defining) us?

2. *Our highest purpose in dealing with these situations.* Given that "every thought, emotion, and behavior is a statement about who we are and who we are becoming," our highest purpose therefore could be to make this statement and/or define ourselves in a purposeful, deliberate way.

3. *What is this statement?* If we were responding to the negative people and situations we encounter in such a way that made a purposeful statement about who we are, what would that statement be, or what

qualities and characteristics would we like to be able to draw upon?

This "clarity of purpose" (the first step in a five-step process) is a critical component of the "Life from the Top of the Mind" perspective, so let's look at these questions one at a time to make sure that we understand it fully and can apply this concept to "real life." For example, what does it mean to become clear about the purpose of the negative situations we encounter on a daily basis? Some people might say that their purpose is to drive us crazy, and while this is understandable, I believe that this interpretation is a big part of the problem. In other words, if our goal is becoming more influential in these challenging situations, then, I think it's pretty easy to see that describing them as if they have the power to "drive us crazy" will not serve that goal.

Like many other professionals in the field of personal productivity, I believe that the language we use to describe ourselves and our world has a significant impact on our experience of life. Therefore, I would never encourage anyone to describe any person or situation as having the power to "drive them crazy." Of course, I'm not suggesting that merely changing our use of language will change our life. In fact, if sustaining this "Top of the Mind" perspective is our goal, we must go much deeper than mere language. In order to change how the negative situations effect us, we must turn the tables and use *them* versus *them* using *us*. This means we must engage these situations in such a way that they support, rather than frustrate our goals.

How do we do this? First, we give them a purpose, or a reason for being that is congruent with what we want to accomplish. A good example of this is a story told by one of my colleagues about a client who came to him complaining about one particular person (a male coworker) who was "driving him crazy." The client was convinced that this coworker was the source of 90% of his misery, and if he could just learn to deal with this person, he would be a happy guy. My colleague immediately agreed to help and began to describe what needed to be done.

"First," he said, *"we will go to the local acting studio and spend some time auditioning actors that look and sound like the person that is bothering you. Next, you will need to write this actor a script, which shouldn't be very difficult because I'm sure you know exactly how he talks and the sort of things he says that bugs you. Then, we will spend approximately six weeks or so practicing with this actor. We will have him come to my office on a weekly basis and, in time, you will learn how to deal with people such as this so that they never again have the power to drive you crazy.*

Of course, you will have to pay the actor for his time, and unfortunately, hiring an actor for six weeks of work will not be cheap . . . or . . . we could do this in a different way. You could practice with the actual, difficult person in your life FOR FREE! I would be working with you, of course, but because you are dealing with this person all the time (and thus getting in a lot of practice), the process won't take nearly as long. In fact, after you have become successful, and therefore immune to people such as this, you can write them a little note thanking him or her for the opportunity to practice."

Another example of giving our daily trials and tribulations a purpose, or using them to practice responding "on purpose," actually happened to me. It began as an invitation to play golf. I am an avid (some might say rabid) fan of the game, and have even created a presentation on its mental and emotional aspects entitled, *"Tee Off or Tee'd Off: The Perils and Problems of Brainstem Golf"* or if you like, simply, *"Golf from the Top of the Mind."*

At some point, I thought it would be a great idea to create a golf excursion where the participants would be able to hear a presentation on how the BRAIN model helps us shift to the neocortex, release muscle tension, and create the sort of mind set that allows us to play our best game. I set everything up at the Banff Springs Hotel in Banff, Canada, and sent out an announcement to those on my mailing list about the trip, and how to sign up.

One of the most interesting responses came from a good friend, and went something like this: *"In reference to your excursion to Banff, I think golf is a white man's elitist's game, and I will have nothing to do with it!"*

As you might imagine, I was at first somewhat taken aback by this response. However, if there is one thing I have learned, it's that if one puts him or herself up as a teacher of dealing with life, then he or she better be able to walk the talk. So, summoning my best thoughts, I responded in this way: *Dear Joe* (not his real name), *Given that I support people in following their beliefs and doing what they feel is right, I support your decision to not participate in the Banff experience."* To which (somewhat tongue in cheek) he replied : *"Hey, when I am trying to be angry with you and you respond in a nice way, it really pisses me off!"* To which I simply responded: *"Thanks for the opportunity to practice."*

The purpose of these stories is to give you at least two examples of what it means to use life (especially the negative aspects of life) versus life using us. When we decide that choosing how we want to define ourselves with respect to a particular situation is our goal, then we can begin to use those situations as opportunities to practice. The reason this is so powerful is that we have given them a purpose, and thus are dealing with them from a more purposeful, deliberate perspective. In other words, we have defined the role they play in our lives and have aligned this purpose/role with what we want to achieve.

Put another way, do you think that you will

ever find yourself dealing with negative people and/ or difficult situations in the future? If the answer to this question is, "yes, of course," how valuable would it be for you to be *in* these situations, but not *of* them. . . to be able to interact with all types of people and/or difficult situations, and yet remain clear, confident, and creative? If this would be an achievement worth your time and effort, then the first step is to imagine that these situations exist for a reason, as if the scenario is a scene in a play, and your purpose is to step on stage and define your character.

Now that we have become clear about the importance of using the negative situations in our lives as opportunities to practice defining ourselves on purpose, the next question, of course, is what should we practice? In my seminars, I allow participants to answer this question for themselves by first listing some of the more problematic "triggers" in their lives, and then determining who they want to be (how do they want to define themselves) when they next encounter these types of situations. The exercise looks something like this:

When Dealing With: (Familiar Triggers)	I would like to Practice being more:
_____	_____
_____	_____
_____	_____

When Dealing With: (Types of People)	I would like to practice: being more:
_____	_____
_____	_____
_____	_____

Just as this is a critically important exercise, it is also critically important that the blanks be filled in by you versus some general list of triggers and suggested responses. This means that if attaining and sustaining this "Top of the Mind" perspective is important to you, then you must decide *when* you want to practice (When Dealing With:_____) and *what* you want to practice (how you want to define yourself in these situations, and/or the statement you wish to make about who you are when dealing with _____).

For this reason, I suggest that you stop and create your own pair of lists. You can do this here in the book, or on a separate piece of paper. Don't worry about getting the "right answer." Either the list of triggers or the qualities you want to practice can always be changed in the future.

Not About "Nots"

This exercise is important, not only because in order to be effective, the list of triggers and desired responses must reflect what is important to you or your experiences, but also because many people initially try to create a solution by merely lessening the problem. In other words, when describing how they want to change, many people will say that they want to be less stressed, less frustrated, angry, etc. This is understandable, however, we now know that holding an image in our mind of what we *don't* want doesn't create what we *do* want. In fact, chances are that this image will actually trigger a chemical reaction similar to that of worry, which only throws our thinking into the lower part of our brain, and often has us producing what we are afraid of (becoming worried about worry or stressed about stress, etc).

An example of this phenomenon is the experience of a small child, say around one and a half to two years old, who spills his milk. Often, because this creates a mess for the parent to clean up, it's not uncommon for the parent to become upset and admonish the child with something like, *"How many times have I told you to be careful with your milk!?! I am going to give you some more, but you'd better not spill it this time!"*

The child, of course is now worried about spilling the milk, and thoughts such as, *"Don't spill the milk. Don't spill the milk"* are likely to be going through his mind. The parent puts a new glass of milk in front of the child, and again tells him what he shouldn't do. *"Okay, now, here is a new glass of milk, you'd better not spill it this time!"* This, of course, only has the child worrying even more about spilling the milk, which makes the internal dialogue of, *"Don't spill the milk. . .don't spill the milk"* even louder and more desperate. It's not hard to predict what happens next. At some point, the child spills the milk. Why? Because the image that is running through his mind is what he is trying to avoid... spilling the milk!

You see, the mind does not register the word "not" with respect to the images it produces. For example, if I were to say to someone: "Do NOT think of a red elephant sitting in front of you," the image that would automatically "spring to mind" would be a red elephant. If they happen to be deathly afraid of red elephants, this would produce a brainstem reaction and a surge of fight-or-flight chemicals, such as adrenaline and cortisol. This is why phobias can be so debilitating. People very understandably try to avoid what frightens them, which only guarantees that they will think about it and be thrown into the brainstem as a result. Again, this has us producing what we fear, such as the child spilling his milk.

Another good example is a golfer setting up to hit a shot near a water hazard. If the internal (and sometimes even external) dialogue is about NOT hitting the ball in the water, you can bet that the next sound will almost always be a splash and a series of curses.

Therefore, this book is not about "nots." Or, put another way, it's not about just avoiding the problem, i.e., becoming less stressed, frustrated, angry etc., because just becoming less worried or stressed does not make us more clear, confident, and creative, or whatever qualities you have identified in terms of who you want to be, and/or what you want to practice.

"When life has tied us in 'nots,'
courage, hope, and optimism
can be our undoing."
Mike Darley

This quote from my friend and philosopher, Mike Darley, illustrates this in a very clever and profound way. There is also another quote that came to me during a session that seems to sum up this philosophy of shifting from avoiding the problem to creating a more purposeful solution. It says:

"When our purpose becomes
avoidance, our life becomes a void."

Therefore, if any of the qualities you described when you were making your list were expressed as what you wanted to avoid, "not this" or "less of that," go back and change them to what you *want*, versus what you are trying to avoid. For example, "less stressed" might really mean more patient, confident, or calm etc.

You have stopped to make your lists, right? If not, here is an easy way to generate the necessary information, or to ensure it is in the proper format to support the changes you desire. Because we think so much of the problems in our lives (more on why this is later), many people find that the list of triggers is easier to come up with than the desired responses. If this is the case, you might want to make your "stressor" list first, and then say:

"When dealing with _____ (deadlines, for example) *I would like to be more* _____ (patient, or focused, again, just an example). "

The important thing to remember in this step is that this isn't how you are "supposed to be," but how, or more importantly "who" you *want* to be in response to the challenging situations you face. Do this for each stressor, and you should be able to generate some idea of how you would like to define yourself, or the statement you want to make about your character in these circumstances.

How ever you do it, just know that until you have a vision of what/who you want to be, or what you want to practice in the challenging situations you face, you will be trapped in the lower part of your brain trying to avoid the problem. Your purpose will be avoidance, which is a fear-based perspective, and you will not be able to access the clarity, confidence, and creativity you desire. This isn't a threat, or something you need to worry about, just good information about what works and what doesn't. Bottom line, just as giving the negative aspects in life a purpose was important in changing our response to them, this is also a critical step in sustaining a "Top of the Mind" perspective.

For those of you who liked the BRAIN model in the first half of the book, you can use it here as well. For example, you can take three to five deep breaths, saying the word "relax" on the exhale which establishes the neocortex as the dominant part of your brain. Then you could change the neocortex question in the "Ask" step of the model from, "How would I rather be feeling?" to "What is my highest purpose here?" or "How do I want to define myself in this situation?" or "What are the qualities or charac-teristics I want to practice as I deal with _____?" You can then imagine bringing these qualities to the situation that in the past, may have been problematic (remember it's your imagination, so you have total control), and then notice how you feel as you use that situation for self-definition, or to make a statement about who you are and who you are becoming.

Let me give you one final illustration to make this step as clear as possible. Let's assume that there is a new television show called, "Life from the Top of the Mind." Twenty participants are chosen from all parts of the country and from all walks of life, and each is taken to a location that is made up of two distinct locales, and are told that this where they will live for the next six months.

The first location is a resort-like atmosphere where the participant is pampered in luxury. They wake up each morning to breakfast in bed if they like, swimming under the palm trees, etc., followed by an hour or two spent with a consultant or support person defining their highest purpose, or the statement they want to make about who they are in "real life." Then, in the afternoon, each participant is taken to an environment that looks exactly like where they live. The homes and office buildings look the same, and even the people they come in contact with in this "artificial" environment look and act exactly like the people back home.

The participants are told that their goal is to go into this environment and "practice" responding to the challenging people and situations they encounter in a way that is congruent with their highest purpose, or the qualities and characteristics they have identified. Their "practice time" is short at first, so that the participants only have to keep their focus for around five minutes. Let's assume that you are one of those participants. Don't you think you could practice responding in a purposeful manner even to the most difficult of situations for five minutes? The next day, the practice time is lengthened to 10 minutes, then to 20 and so on, until by the end of the six month period, the participant is spending almost the entire day practicing responding on purpose.

Can you see how, after six months of practicing responding in this purposeful way, you will likely become very good at this way of life? Further, can you see how after this extended period of practice, you would be able to return to your life and continue to respond in this more purposeful manner?

Of course, there is good news and bad news. The bad news is that we don't have a network or production company to create an environment in which we can practice, and the good news is that we don't need one. We already have it available to us . . . it's called life! You see, life will always give us plenty of opportunities to practice. We will either practice responding in the old ways we have identified (the cycle of stress) . . . or we will practice responding in the new ways we have identified as congruent with our highest purpose.

This . . .   Or This!

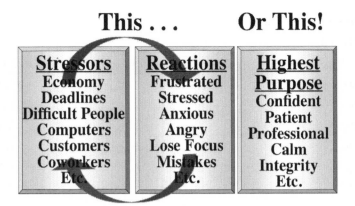

Stressors	Reactions	Highest Purpose
Economy	Frustrated	Confident
Deadlines	Stressed	Patient
Difficult People	Anxious	Professional
Computers	Angry	Calm
Customers	Lose Focus	Integrity
Coworkers	Mistakes	Etc.
Etc.	Etc.	

My guess is that we don't need to practice the old responses because we are already pretty good at them! In other words, if we ever need to respond to life with stress, frustration, or resentment, we will have no trouble because we have been practicing these responses for quite some time. Our more purposeful qualities, on the other hand, might take some practice. The thing to remember is this:

We are always practicing something!

There is no neutral experience. If we are not practicing on purpose, we will be continuing to react to life in old habitual ways, and thus practice reinforcing the old responses that seem to come so naturally. Therefore, I suggest that we use life versus life using us, and make the more challenging experiences in life (if not all experiences) opportunities to practice defining ourselves in a way that is congruent with our highest purpose, which, by the way, is also congruent with living "life from the top of the mind."

For example, if you look at the responses identified as part of the cycle of stress, it's pretty easy to see how these (frustration, stress, resentment, etc.) are "fight-or-flight" in nature, and thus arise from our brainstem. By the same token, if you look at the qualities of clarity, confidence, and creativity (plus those more purposeful characteristics you identified earlier as your highest purpose), you can easily see how these come from the "top of our mind," or our neocortex. In fact, this is yet another way to use our knowledge of how the brain works to make choices about how we respond. We can always use neocortex criteria and/or neocortex questions to determine whether to hold on to our thoughts, emotions, and behavior, or whether to change them. Therefore, at this point, I would like to introduce another model consisting of four, powerful neocortex questions which are designed to support you in bringing this "Top of the Mind" perspective to life. I call these questions *"The Four Criteria,"* and after introducing them here, I will attempt to integrate these neocortex questions into the rest of the book.

The Four Criteria:

1. Was this thought, emotion and/or behavior chosen deliberately or "on purpose?" Meaning, did you decide that thinking/feeling this way was a

good idea?

2. Is it working for you? Meaning, is this thought, emotion, or behavior helping you create the experience of life you want?

3. Is it making the statement you want to make about who you are?

And my favorite...

4. Would you teach this thought, emotion, and/or behavior to a child, and/or someone you love?

Given that these are all neocortex questions (or questions that can only be answered by the upper 80% of our brain), they are almost guaranteed to engage our best thoughts and produce a "Top of the Mind" response. Further, I believe that these questions can be applied to any situation, and thus should serve us very well as we use life versus life using us by seeing all people and situations as an opportunity to practice.

In fact, you can combine these questions with the BRAIN Model to make it even more effective. In other words, rather than just asking "How would I rather be feeling?" you can breathe deeply (using the 4-4-4 method), say the word "relax" on the exhale, and ask yourself:

1. Am I reacting to life on purpose?
2. How's it working for me?

3. Is this the way I want to be defined?
4. Would I teach and/or recommend this way of being to someone I love?

If the answer to any of these questions is "No!" then you can use them to shift from clarity about the problem to clarity about the solution. In other words, you can ask,

If I were responding to life on purpose, in a way that is more effective, in a way that defines who I am, and in a way I would recommend to someone I love, what would that look like (What qualities and/or characteristics would meet this new criteria)?

You then imagine bringing this new way of being to the situation (to life) and notice the changes.

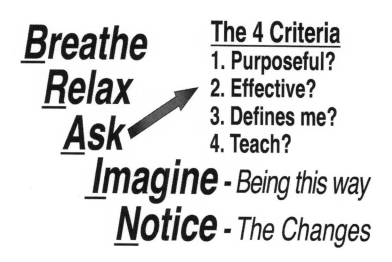

Breathe
Relax
Ask

The 4 Criteria
1. Purposeful?
2. Effective?
3. Defines me?
4. Teach?

Imagine - *Being this way*
Notice - *The Changes*

People tell me that these four questions are invaluable in making decisions, in general, and therefore, I encourage you to put them in your phone, or some place where you can access them easily and refer to them as often as possible.

Of course, while valuable, the idea of identifying who you want to be, and seeing life as an opportunity to practice implementing this self-definition is only the first step of a more inclusive, five-step model. Let's continue to the second step to understand what is the true cause of our emotions and behaviors, and how we can have more influence in our experience of life.

CHAPTER 10

Clarity About Our Past

If you remember, the second part of this book is based upon the C³ Model of Clarity, Confidence, and Creativity, and we began by becoming clear about the importance of dealing with the negative aspects of life "on purpose." Now we must become clear about why we find ourselves stuck in the Cycle of Frustration & Stress in the first place, and how we can use this knowledge to align our thoughts, emotions, and behavior with who we want to be. In other words, we must become clear about the true cause of why we think, feel, and act in certain ways, and what we can do to become more influential in this process.

From my perspective, there are two principle

causes, and the first is "our past." When I refer to our past, I mean any old habits, tendencies, beliefs, and/or learned perspectives that may be incongruent with our highest purpose. Let's face it. Our past is where we learned who we were, or were expected to be. Our past is also where we learned how to react to situations and other people in general. Basically, our past is where we learned what the world was like, and our place in this world.

It didn't matter that "the world" we saw was mostly what went on in our family. In fact, most of us didn't think, "This is just how my family is." We just thought, "This is how the world is," and from this experience, we formed our core beliefs, habitual ways of reacting to the world, preconceptions of life, etc. And, in many ways, we continue to repeat these habitual ways of being today. This shouldn't be surprising. The reason they call them habits is because they're habitual, which means we seem to find ourselves behaving and reacting without our conscious thought.

Don't get me wrong. I'm not saying that everything, or even most of what we learned from our past is bad or wrong, or even incongruent with our purpose. I'm sure that some of what you learned serves you very well today, and that you may want to hold on to this aspect of your past. The good news is that you will (hold onto what you learned, that is). The reason I can say this with such certainty is because this learning has taken the form of a habit or core belief. This doesn't mean that we can't change our core beliefs if we find they are incongruent with our purpose. It just means that we may want to hold on to some of our learning, and, if this is the case, we needn't do a thing because it is woven into the fabric of who we have become.

For example, I remember something that I learned from my past that is very congruent with, or supportive of, my purpose today. If you remember, I described my past as growing up in the home of a recovering alcoholic. Both my mom and dad were very active in the programs of Alcoholics Anonymous and Al Anon, and, from as early as I can remember, our lives revolved around going to meetings and interacting with other people and families in the program.

Our kitchen table was a place that people would come on a regular basis to pour their hearts out and, often, turn their lives around. Dad was always talking to someone on the phone, going out in the middle of the night on "twelve-step calls," and attending AA meetings. In fact, as I mentioned earlier, we went to meetings so often it was almost like going to McDonald's to me, because I remember playing around the meeting halls and watching my mom and dad stand up in front of all those people and tell their story, over and over again.

Consequently, I have never had a fear of public speaking. In my studies, I have learned that this is one of the most common of all our fears, more so than snakes, or heights, or even death! However, because I saw my parents speak at AA meetings on a regular basis, it never even occurred to me that speaking to large groups of people was something to be afraid of. In fact, I have a tape of myself at the age of five speaking at an AA meeting, and while I can't make out what I was saying, I was clearly saying it with confidence because I had watched my mom and dad do this so often.

Given that this has been such a natural part of my growing up and learning about the world, to this day, I have never imagined that speaking in front of a group of five hundred or five thousand was anything to be frightened of. In other words, this part of my past, or the legacy that was given to me by my mother and father, is very congruent with my purpose. I didn't learn it "on purpose," however it serves me very well today. In fact, as a speaker, trainer, and counselor, this experience of growing up in this type of environment has given me a model for communicating and helping that has served me well, and continues to be a resource for my ability to be effective in those roles. In many ways, I am very grateful that I grew up in this type of AA household. That's the good news.

The bad news is that Dad seemed to use home as a place to recharge his batteries. When he was speaking at an AA meeting, he was "up" and "on" and "alive." Similarly, at home, when someone would call from AA, he would light up, and be full of all kinds of energy and enthusiasm. The rest of the time, however, he would sit and watch TV or sleep (at least, this is how I remember it). I have very few memories of him interacting with mom and me with the same enthusiasm or intensity that he gave to those he was helping in A.A. I never remember being upset about this. . . it just seemed to be "the way things were." Almost as if there was an unspoken rule that Dad's sobriety was essential for the stability of the family, and the way that Dad stayed sober was through A.A. Therefore, whatever supported this was essential.

Just to be clear, I want you to understand that I didn't, and still don't, see A.A., or Dad's involvement in A.A. as the problem. Quite the contrary, I see my exposure to the power of this twelve-step program as one of the most beneficial aspects of my childhood... one that continues to be a very positive influence in my work today and very congruent with my highest purpose.

What I am saying is that my memory of my father (and therefore my belief about what it means to be a father) was of someone who was very outgoing, nurturing, and supportive of those he came in contact with outside the family... and, somebody who used his home as a place to recharge his batteries, which means that he didn't give the same energy to his loved ones that he gave to others.

Of course, I never remember saying to myself, "That's how I am going to be when I grow up." However (as you might have guessed), as I entered my late twenties and early thirties, I found myself drawn to speaking and counseling (surprise, surprise). I even earned a master's degree in counseling psychology and was working toward my Ph.D., and . . . guess what? I found myself speaking to large groups of people with relative ease, and with a great deal of enthusiasm (just like my dad). In addition, when I was working with someone in counseling, I found myself very focused and enthusiastic about helping them (just like my dad). Then, I would go home and (you guessed it), recharge my batteries (just like my dad).

Finally, as my style of counseling, or my way of working with others, became increasingly focused on helping them be more purposeful in their lives, I began to examine my own life in terms of this paradigm (what a novel idea). As I did, I discovered this discrepancy. Clearly, following this old learned perspective of using home as a place to just recharge my batteries was incongruent with my purpose, a big part of which was to be a loving and present force in my relationship with my wife and children.

As I became aware of this, I was able to change ("Problems cannot be solved at the same level of awareness that created them." Albert Einstein). Now, when I come home, I purposefully give loving attention to my wife, Georgia, and my two sons, Chris and Nik. Not because "I'm supposed to," but because it's congruent with my highest purpose, and defines me in a way or makes a statement about who I am that I can be proud of. If I need to rest after a particularly exhausting presentation or trip, I say, "Dad needs a nap!" and I go take a short nap. You see, I still use home as a place to recharge my batteries, I just do this in a purposeful way, or a way that is congruent with or how I want to define myself as a husband, father, speaker, and counselor.

That's the nice thing about becoming very clear about what our life would look like if we were living "on purpose." Once we have done this, we can use this vision as a criteria to determine which aspects of our past (which habits, learned perspectives, etc.) we want to hold on to, and which ones we want to let go of, or better yet change, so that our new habits are congruent with our highest purpose.

Just as I have a tendency to look forward to speaking in public versus fearing it, I'm sure that there are habits and learned ways of being that you want to hang on to as well. However, I think that we can all acknowledge that there are also learned ways of reacting to life that do not serve us and that we would not like to hold on to and/or teach to those we love.

With respect to living life from the top of the mind, these less than desirable reactions can probably be seen on the right side of the Cycle of Stress.

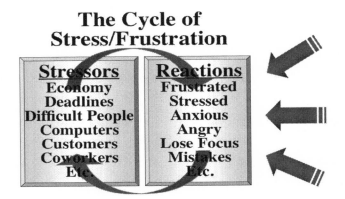

What it is important to recognize here is that these are learned reactions. We didn't come out of the womb reacting to exams with anxiety and difficult instructors with resentment. Further, as we have already established, we didn't learn to react in these negative ways "on purpose." And yet, learn them we did. Therefore, unless we challenge them and change them, they will continue to influence our experience of life, even if that experience is negative.

The power of these old learned habits and perspectives was demonstrated very convincingly by Martin Seligman, Ph.D., a psychologist who was initially known for his work on the concept of what he called "learned helplessness."

In 1965, Seligman, while a graduate student in the department of experimental psychology at the University of Pennsylvania, performed the first experiment showing that animals can be taught "helplessness." One group of dogs was given an "escapable shock," meaning, by pushing a panel with its nose, any dog in that group could terminate or turn off the shock. A second group of dogs was given exactly the same shocks as the first, but they had no way to stop the shock and couldn't escape. A third "control group" was given no shocks at all.

Once the dogs went through the experiment, each was put in a large box with two compartments separated by a low wall. In the first compartment they received a shock, but they could easily escape the shock by jumping over the barrier into the other side of the box. Within seconds, the dogs that had learned that they could control the previous shocks jumped over the barrier and escaped. The dogs that earlier had received no shocks did the same thing, also in a matter of seconds. But two thirds of the dogs who had been taught that they had no control, that nothing they did mattered, made no effort to escape, even though they could easily see over the low barrier to the shockless zone of the box. Those dogs just gave up and lay down, even though they were being regularly shocked by the box.

Dr. Seligman concluded that the reason two thirds of the dogs from the second group made no attempt to escape is because they had previously learned that they were helpless. Therefore, when they found themselves in a similar situation, they reacted based upon this learned perspective of helplessness versus jumping to the other side of the box.

Unfortunately, I think we all may have to deal with a bit of "learned helplessness," because there was a time in our lives when we were truly helpless. As children, there were many situations which we could neither change nor leave, and thus we may have some preconceptions about ourselves and the world that reinforce this helplessness rather than our power to change.

In fact, these old learned ways of responding aren't just thoughts, they are actual physical pathways in our brain. You see, whenever we think something, feel something, or do something, we create and/or reinforce what are known as neural pathways.

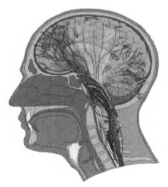

These conduits are similar to pathways in the woods in that, if they are new, they may be hard to find and go down. However, if we have reacted this way for a long time, the pathways are well worn, easy to find, and easy to go down.

That's why the reactions of stress, anxiety, frustration, and anger are so common and so easily triggered. The good news, however, is that we can begin to create and strengthen new neural pathways that go up to the neocortex versus down to the brainstem. These will be like new pathways in the woods at first. However, as we continue to practice thinking, feeling, and acting in ways that we would recommend to someone we love, we will begin to reinforce these new, more purposeful ways of being.

This is one of the reasons I have chosen to write this book, and the good news is that you have just taken a major step toward dispelling this old belief that nothing can be done (i.e. identified a more purposeful way of being when dealing with life's challenges). The bad news is that these will remain just good ideas, and eventually fade from awareness if we don't deepen our understanding of what actually causes us to think, feel, and behave the way we do and practice this new way of being. Put another way, if you want to have more influence over your emotions, behavior, and overall experience of life (and to some degree the emotions, behavior, and experience of others) then we need to understand the causal factors behind each.

CHAPTER 11

Clarity About
What Causes
Our Emotions

Most people think it's the facts, or what happens to us that makes us feel and act in certain ways. While the facts do play some role, I'm going to suggest that it's actually our beliefs (perceptions, interpretations, and expectations) that are the most influential factors in determining our emotions, behaviors, and experience of life.

Let me give you an example. A long time ago, most people believed that the earth was flat. Based upon this belief, when a ship sailed out and didn't come back, most people thought that it had fallen off the edge of the earth. In other words, the prevailing belief that the world was flat influenced how the data (the ship not returning to port) was interpreted. Further, it's very likely that these same people would expect that if another ship sailed out too far, it would also fall off of the edge.

Here we have an excellent example of a belief coloring how data is interpreted, and the combination (of the belief and interpretation) creating an expectation about the future. Staying with our example, when people thought that ships were falling off of the edge of the earth (based upon their belief that the earth was flat), and their expectation that this would continue to happen if the ships sailed out too far, they would very likely be afraid of sailing on ships, at least on the ships that were going to venture out of sight of the shoreline. Based upon this emotion (fear), they would understandably avoid ships (a behavior) which would produce a positive experience of feeling safe because they are not putting themselves in danger of falling off of the edge of the world. The graphic below demonstrates how this happens.

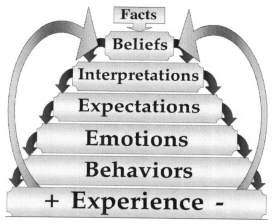

The facts (or what happens to us) are filtered through our beliefs. These beliefs then create our interpretations which then create our expectations. Of course, because all of this happens so fast (and in the unconscious part of the brain), we don't experience it this way. However, it is important to understand what is going on if we want to be able to influence the process. Plus, as we have seen, the expectation that was created by our beliefs and interpretations is generally experienced as a worrisome image of some sort (such as ships sailing over the edge of the world). The reason this is important is that we have already learned that any image we hold in our mind produces certain chemical effects in our body, whether it's happening or not (remember the lemon?).

This is one of the reasons why emotions are so hard to change. First, they (emotions) have been produced by beliefs and interpretations that we think are "true" (of course the earth is flat, of course deadlines make me anxious, of course difficult people make me angry, etc.). Secondly, they create images of what we expect to happen next (I will stay anxious until the deadline passes, I will either have to make the difficult person change or remove them from my life before I can find any peace of mind). We don't see the emotion as a result of the belief/interpretation. We think it is being caused by the negative situation.

The ABC model developed by Dr. Albert Ellis can be helpful in understanding what is truly going on here. If we were to call the negative events and/or people in our lives, "A" (for the "adverse event") and how we react to theses events/people, "C" for the "consequences," we can see how most people believe that A causes C.

Most People Believe
A ▪▪ ➡ C

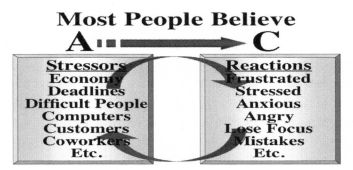

Stressors	Reactions
Economy	Frustrated
Deadlines	Stressed
Difficult People	Anxious
Computers	Angry
Customers	Lose Focus
Coworkers	Mistakes
Etc.	Etc.

Of course, the problem with this belief is that in order to feel differently, we must change "A," or somehow change all of the negative people and events to positive ones to ensure that they will no longer cause us pain. Suffice it to say, if you have made it this far in the book, you know that this isn't a viable solution.

In fact, we now know that the reason we have reacted with frustration or anger in the past was because the middle part of our brain (our limbic system) saw (interpreted) these events/people as problematic or threatening. This interpretation threw our thinking into our brainstem, and we become trapped in the lower 20%, producing chemicals such as adrenaline and cortisol, and limiting our responses to fight-or-flight (the cycle of stress/frustration).

This awareness allows us to reject the premise that "A," or the adverse event causes "C," (the consequences). This is the good news because it means that we don't have to change "A," or the negative events in our life to be able to influence "C," (how we react). The reason that this is the case is because "A" doesn't cause "C". "A" is filtered through or triggers "B," and "B" causes "C," and, of course, "B" is our beliefs. (More on why this is the goods news later.)

Using the analogy introduced earlier, ships falling off the edge of the earth didn't cause people to be fearful of sailing. What caused them to be afraid was their belief that the earth was flat, and thus all ships that sailed out too far would fall off the edge.

A is Filtered Through B
& B Causes C

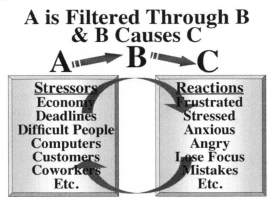

This is a relatively new (and some might even say radical) perspective, so let me give you another example of how this works. Let's say that we have three people in a room. The first was bitten by a dog when she was small, and has been afraid of dogs ever since. The second person in the room loves dogs. She has eight to ten dogs at home, and thinks dogs are one of the most loving of God's creations. The third person is from a country where dogs don't exist, and thus, he has never seen a dog before in his life.

You bring a dog into the room (fact). Predictably, you will see three very different reactions based upon three different sets of beliefs, interpretations, and expectations.

1. The person who believes that dogs are dangerous interprets this as a dangerous situation. Her expectation is that she will be hurt. Her emotion is fear, and her behavior is to run from the room.

2. The person who believes that dogs are lovable joyfully exclaims, "A dog!" and goes over to pet and hug the dog. She interprets the situation as an opportunity to interact with one of her favorite animals, and her expectation is that she gets to be licked by the dog. Obviously, her emotion, behavior, and experience is positive.

3. The person who has never seen a dog before is confused, and just stands there wondering, "What the heck is that?" Not being able to draw any conclusions from his colleagues (one ran *away* from it, and the other ran *toward* this strange animal), he doesn't know what to do.

So, here you have a fact (a dog is brought into a room) resulting in three different sets of interpretations, expectations, emotions, and behaviors. However, IT'S THE SAME DOG, which means it can't be the situation itself causing the response. What *is* causing the reactions are the individuals' beliefs about dogs, and again, this is the good news. Why? Because, if our goal is to become more influential in how we feel, what we do, and generally how we experience life, we have much more influence over our beliefs than we do any other aspect of the situation.

Unfortunately, this is not what most of us have been taught. Most of us were raised to believe that it's what happens to us (the facts) that cause us to react in specific ways, and thus we have been practicing or living by this belief for quite a while. In fact, many people have become so used to living this way that they are afraid of changing. They may even think of this way of life as a "comfort zone" from which they do not want to stray. However, if you have ever experienced the "cycle of stress/frustration," you know that it's not a very "comfortable" zone or place to be.

Still, you may know people who cling to the beliefs that create this experience of life, even though the result is anything but comforting. There is a great quote by Michael Levine that explains this phenomena very well that says:

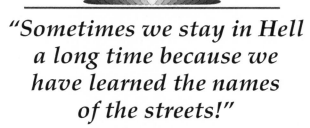

"Sometimes we stay in Hell a long time because we have learned the names of the streets!"

Michael Levine

I love this quote because it so succinctly explains why we keep doing the same thing over and over, even if doesn't seem to be working for us. We have "learned the names of the streets," meaning that this reaction has become so habitual and ingrained that we keep making the same judgements (which produce the same reactions), not because they are particularly comfortable or even effective, but because they are familiar.

In other words, it's not our "comfort zone" because it's not that comfortable. Instead, I call it our "known zone." It's what has become "known" or familiar, which explains why much of the material in this book, while compelling, might seem radical and even a bit unsettling to some because they have been taught to fear the unknown or unfamiliar.

By the way, have you noticed that the words "familiar" and "familial" are very similar? To be clear, I am not trying to blame our parents or our past for the habitual way we have learned to react to life. I just want you to understand why attempting to change these reactions, and shifting to a "Top of the Mind" perspective may seem awkward or hard at first. Just as learning any new skill, at first it will very likely feel unfamiliar. In fact, given the power of language, the word "unfamiliar" is a good way to describe the less than comfortable feelings (doubt, second guessing yourself, etc.), you may experience as you learn to live from the "Top of the

Mind." Why? Because describing the experience this way automatically makes room for the fact that as we become more familiar with the process, it will seem more natural, and will eventually become a more purposeful habit. The challenge, of course, is to hang in there or practice this new way of being long enough for this to come to pass.

Of course, as mentioned earlier, we are always practicing something, and that's why this model for success begins with *clarity*, clarity about what we want to practice (our highest purpose) and what we don't, the old habits, beliefs, preconceptions, and/or learned perspectives that are incongruent with this purpose.

As we have discovered, the most powerful of these are our beliefs, for they give birth to everything else. In fact, the term "preconception" refers to a concept (belief) or conceptualization (way of interpreting or conceptualizing data) that has been created in the past (hence the prefix "pre."). Plus, the word conception means "to give birth." So, if we want to bring certain qualities to life, we must be very purposeful with respect to the concepts or beliefs that drive this creative process.

To make this decision, we must first be aware of the beliefs themselves, especially those that are associated with the aspects of our lives that in the past, we would have defined as "stressors." Therefore, I suggest that you take a moment and look at the list you made in Chapter Nine, i.e., those situations and types of people that have been problematic (or just make a new list now). Whether it was deadlines, certain types of difficult people, traffic, your job, the amount of money in your bank account, or anything else that has seemed to "cause your stress" in the past, let's put them in their place and identify these as "A" or "the adverse event(s)." This will then allow you to identify "B," or the belief you have about these events or people, and "C" the consequence of holding on to this belief as valid, and allowing it to drive your thoughts, emotions, and behaviors.

To identify these beliefs, you can use this template and fill in the blanks:

In the past, I reacted to ____A____ (the identified stressor, such as deadlines, traffic, difficult people, etc.) with ____C____ (the old response, such as stressed, worried, frustrated, etc.) because I was concerned or afraid that ____B____ (your reasoning or rationale of the problem) might occur.

Or if you like, it could be written as, "In the past, when I faced ____A____ (the stressor), I was concerned that ____B____ (your worry or concern), which made me feel ____C____ (the negative response) might happen.

Basically, anytime we can put, "I'm afraid that . . ." (or "worried that . . .," or "concerned that

. . .") in any sentence, we know we are processing this information from the brainstem, and unless the situation is fight-or-flight in nature, we will not be accessing the most intelligent, purposeful part of our brain. Still, the first step to change is awareness of the causal belief, and therefore we can use the template suggested earlier to understand how these old perspectives have affected us in the past.

For example, if someone had a problem with deadlines, they might write:

"In the past, when I faced a deadline (A), I was afraid that (B), my missing the deadline, would result in my being seen as less than competent, letting my team down, being reprimanded or even fired, etc., and so I felt (C), worried and stressed, until the deadline passed."

What this illustrates is a brainstem belief about deadlines, i.e., that they are something to be feared because of their potential to make this person look bad or even lose his or her job. While this belief is understandable and maybe even common, it is just that, a belief, perspective, or preconception about deadlines that is coming from the lower 20% of their brain. If it were a fact, everyone would experience the situation the same way.

For example, if anyone jumps off of a 20-story building without a parachute, they will fall and quickly come into contact with the ground, with rather disastrous results. This will happen no matter what the jumper believes about his or her ability to fly. With deadlines, however, this isn't the case. In fact, some people actually say that they work best with a deadline. They see this as good information about when a project needs to be finished, and use this information to plan out what needs to be done. The only difference between the two scenarios is the way that the information is perceived or interpreted (which we now know depends on what part of the brain is processing the information). This is the power of beliefs, and why becoming aware of these perspectives is a key component to becoming influential in our lives.

Interestingly enough, many people resist this explanation and cling to the thought that, "No! It's the negative situations that make me feel bad!" Of course, given the power of beliefs, if this is how they choose to explain or conceptualize their experience of life, then this will be true for them. Unfortunately, if they hold on to this belief, the only way they can change their experience will be to change the world around them, and they may find that many of the negative events and people in their life resist being changed. Plus, as we have learned, those who see problems as problematic (and thus cause their limbic system to send the data to the brainstem and trigger worry and stress) will quickly become trapped in this lower 20% of their brain, as well as be limited in their attempt to influence the quality of their lives.

As mentioned earlier, if we don't want to give negative events and / or people the power to "make us" feel one way or another, then we must take control of that power ourselves. The first step in this process is to see these negative reactions for what they are... chemical changes in our body that result from our becoming trapped in our brainstem. Next, we must be able to shift from our brainstem to the "top of our mind," and change the chemical makeup of our body. This is the function of the BRAIN model introduced in the first part of the book.

Having accomplished this, we must be willing to use life versus life using us, which means consulting our neocortex to determine how we want to define ourselves, or the statement we want to make about who we are when we are dealing with these challenging events and people. This means that rather than stating a belief that leaves us trapped in our brainstem, such as, "I am a person who becomes stressed when dealing with deadlines, or frustrated around certain kinds of people," we can go back to the list of qualities and characteristics we came up with in Chapter Nine about the "Clarity of Purpose," and restate:

When I am dealing with _____,

I want to practice _____.

Or, we can actually put this belief in the form of a purposeful, self-defining statement by saying something like, *"I am a person who is practicing patience* (or confidence, or whatever quality you have chosen) *when dealing with difficult people, deadlines, etc."* Once we have this vision, and are willing to see the negative situations in our lives as opportunities to practice, we must become aware of any old beliefs, habits, and/or preconceptions that are incongruent with this higher purpose. Remember the quote from Albert Einstein, *"Problems cannot be solved at the same level of awareness that created them?"* This means that we must raise our awareness as to whether the beliefs we have learned are serving us.

Again, one way to do this is to look at the negative reactions we have had to situations and/or certain types of people in our past, and determine what old beliefs/interpretations caused these reactions. For example, we could say, "In the past, I became frustrated or angry with people who drove too slow or too fast in traffic because I was worried that _____ (they would keep me from getting where I wanted to go on time, they would cause an accident or were "beating me," and not playing by the rules, etc.) In this example, we can see how our beliefs defined us, because this tendency to react to slow drivers could also be stated as, *"In the past, I was a person who regularly became frustrated with people who drove too slow or too fast."*

Now we apply "The Four Criteria" to determine whether we want to hang on to this perspective:

1. Was this belief/reaction chosen on purpose?
2. Is it working for me?
3. Is this the statement I want to make about who I am in response to this situation?
4. Would I recommend this belief to someone I loved or teach it to a child?

As you can see, when this higher, "Top of the Mind" criteria is applied, the answer is clear. Further, now we are in the position to create a new way of interpreting the speed people happen to be driving by stating: *"From now on, I am going to practice bringing the quality of _____ (serenity, acceptance, patience, etc.) to my experience of people who happen to be driving slower or faster than I am.* Or, *"I am practicing becoming a person who responds to slow or fast drivers with _____."*

In addition to the power of beliefs, there are linguistic forces at work here as well. As mentioned earlier, I am a person who believes that the language we use to define ourselves and our lives has a powerful impact on our experience, and thus for those of us who want to maximize our ability to effect this experience, I suggest we use the proper tense in this description. For example, some people will state, *"I really get anxious when I have to deal with deadlines."* What is important to notice about this statement is that it is framed in the present tense. However, I would bet that at the moment they aren't dealing with a deadline, and thus the statement isn't accurate. What they really mean is "in the past" they became anxious when they were under some sort of deadline. Notice the difference in these two statements? The second starts off with the words "in the past." Not only is this more accurate (in that it isn't happening in the present), these three words can actually pave the way for a more purposeful statement about who we want to be from this moment on.

For example, the phrase, *"In the past, I had a tendency to become anxious when dealing with deadlines."* makes way for something like, *"From now on, I want to practice patience, confidence, and creativity when given a time by which a project must be completed,"* or *"From now on, I am going to practice being a person who sees deadlines as good information and responds accordingly."*

Of course, these are my words, and the way you phrase the statement might be different. What's important here aren't the specific words, but (a) the tense we use to describe what is happening ("in the past" versus "from now on," and (b) the fact that we are making a purposeful statement about who we are, and what we want to practice.

For those of you who want to know how all of this works in our brains, let's go back to the illustration of the brainstem, limbic system, and neocortex.

As we have discussed, data comes in through our five senses, and is first scanned by our limbic system.

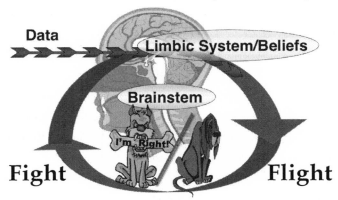

Because the limbic system is the part of the brain that is supposed to determine whether the data we are receiving is dangerous or some sort of a threat, this is also the part of the brain that holds our beliefs about exactly what is threatening and what isn't. Often, the criteria for this decision is determined by what we have found problematic or threatening in the past, and thus exists as a preconception. For example, the person who had been bitten by a dog, is operating from the belief that dogs are dangerous (now and forever), and thus interpreted the fact that a dog had been brought into the room as a threat.

Again, this reinforces the power of our beliefs and the importance of interpreting incoming data in a purposeful (versus habitual) manner. If our old beliefs about a particular situation and / or person are negative, the limbic system will immediately send the data about this stimuli down to the brainstem, bypassing our neocortex.

As we now know, this triggers a release of adrenaline, noradrenaline, and cortisol, which sends our body into a fight-or-flight mode. Further, because we then try to deal with whatever situation we are facing from this hypertensive state, we actually become less and less effective. This only increases our stress and frustration, and we become trapped in the lower 20% of the brain.

There is a story you may have heard that illustrates how different parts of our brain can produce different experiences of life. It's about a little boy who was getting into a lot of fights at school. He was confused because a part of him believed that you should stand up for yourself, and not take any "lip" from anyone, while another part of him knew that fighting really wasn't the way to solve problems.

Unfortunately, however, he had not resolved these two perspectives, and thus was constantly getting into fights. Further, his teachers, and parents were becoming increasingly upset and concerned about the problem, and so finally the little boy went to talk to his grandfather. He said, *"Grandfather, I don't know what to do. I'm getting into a lot of fights at school, and part of me says not to take any lip from anyone while another part says that fighting isn't the way to solve problems. I am really confused."* His grandfather was very wise, and therefore, rather than lecturing to the boy, he told him a story about himself. He said, *"You know, I felt exactly the same way when I was your age. It was like I had these two dogs inside of me . . . one was a mean, old dog, always looking to pick a fight, and the other was a more intelligent, even friendly dog, and they always seemed to be struggling for dominance."*

Upon hearing this, the boy's eyes lit up, and he said:

"That's it! That's it! Which dog won?"

The grandfather took a moment to let the message he was about to deliver sink in, and then very quietly said:

"It depended on which dog I fed."

What I love about this story is how it reminds us that we are always feeding one of two dogs. We are feeding the "underdog" (the brainstem / undermind) or the "top dog" (our neocortex / Top of the Mind), and the dog that we feed, or the part of the brain to which we consistently send data will be the part of the brain that dominates our thinking and our life.

> *"It's not what we feel but what we feed that determines our experience of life."*
> *Bill Crawford*

This is why we must be very purposeful about how we interpret the data we receive from our five senses when dealing with the more "challenging" aspects of life. If we see the data as problematic, something to worry about, a threat, or "awful" in some way, we will feed the underdog, flood our body with stress-related chemicals, limit our ability to respond, and block access to the more intelligent part of our brain. On the other hand, if we are willing to interpret the data as "good information," we engage the neocortex and actually broaden or increase our options and build on the skills we already have.

Basically, the choice is between seeing the situation as either a problem or good information about a solution. Obviously, I suggest the latter. For example, we are stuck in traffic . . . good information. Rather than cursing the drivers around us or ourselves for not anticipating this predicament, we may want to call ahead and let whomever we are meeting know what's happening. We may want to rethink our departure time and/or morning routine so that we give ourselves more time in the future, or take another route. Or, we may want to just accept that this will take a certain amount of time, and decide how we want to use this part of our life. We might want to listen to a book on tape, or a certain piece of music. In other words use this time "on purpose."

We are facing a deadline . . . good information. Rather than worrying about what will happen if we don't finish the project on time, we can ensure that we have planned out what needs to be done, and how long it will take. If, after a thorough assessment of the time line, we determine that the deadline cannot be met, we can communicate this information (in a clear, confident, and creative way), to the party responsible for setting the deadline, and determine what sort of flexibility they have. However, even if there is no flexibility, we can continue to do our best work knowing that we have given them our best thoughts on the feasibility of the project, and that our responsibility is to turn in work that makes a statement about who we are.

Bottom line, in order to use the data we receive from our five senses (versus it using us), we must hold the belief that all information is "good information" (or at least valuable information). This will send the data up to the "Top of our Mind," and allow us to use it to inform who we are, and what we do in the present and future.

The easiest way to do this is to begin with clarity, and go into the situation clear about (a) our highest purpose (the qualities and characteristics we want to practice, and/or the statement we want to make about who we are), (b) our past, or the validity and value of the old habits and beliefs we have been practicing to date.

In this way, we will be forming a conceptualization of what has happened and what is about to happen "on purpose" and from the more purposeful part of our brain, versus allowing our old worries and fears (brainstem) to dominate our thinking. This ability to know who we are and what we want to practice before we enter a situation should serve us very well.

Of course, this can be a tall order because, as mentioned earlier, this way of thinking is likely to be new and "unfamiliar" to most of us. In fact, for a while, it is very likely that we will still find ourselves reacting to the world in old, predictable ways in some situations. No problem... following what we have learned, we can see this reaction as "good information," meaning that we can use the stress/frustration as a valuable signal. ("Stress is a signal something needs to change.") At this point, we can stop and allow our neocortex to regain control by taking three to five deep breaths and saying the word "relax" on the exhale, and ask the kind of "Top of the Mind" questions that allow us to access our best thinking, such as, "Who do I want to be (how do I want to define myself) in response to this situation? What are the old beliefs/interpretations that are causing me to feel frustrated? How is this data good information? What would I recommend to someone I cared for in this situation?

Then, having become clear about our purpose and our past, we can move forward, confident in the knowledge that the upper 80% of our brain is driving our thoughts decisions, and behaviors, and that we are on our way to learning how to live "life from the top of the mind."

Because this is such a new way of thinking and being, however, I want to give you as many tools as possible to support you in your success. Therefore, let's continue to add to this second model, which, if you remember, is designed to allow you to not only create a "Top of the Mind" perspective, but maintain it, even while dealing with life's most challenging situations.

Since this book was first published, I have added a new concept to this part of the model which is designed to give you yet another way of remembering and applying these ideas.

I call it "Owning Our Piece of the P.I.E." By this, I mean taking responsibility for the Perceptions, Interpretations, and Expectations that play such a large role in how we experience life. It's basically another way to become more purposeful with respect to our beliefs, however, for some, this more specific way of describing how we think about ourselves and the world has proven to be helpful.

To "own our piece of the P.I.E." so to speak, we can ask, "Are my perceptions, interpretations, and expectations about a particular situation serving me?" "Are they helping me create the life I want?" "Would I recommend them to someone I loved?" Then, only continue when the answer is "Yes."

CHAPTER 12

Clarity About
The Wisdom of
Serenity

O f course, we are still talking about the value of the C³ lifestyle, or how to bring clarity, confidence, and creativity to everything we do. Thus, the third step in this new model is called Clarity About The Wisdom of Serenity." This concept should be familiar to you in that it was mentioned earlier in the book in conjunction with the word "Relax" in the BRAIN model.

If you remember, the "serenity" I am referring to here is based upon the "Serenity Prayer," attributed to the Protestant theologian, Reinhold

Niebuhr, which states, "God grant me the serenity to accept the things I cannot change, the courage to change the things I can, and the wisdom to know the difference."

Earlier, in Part One, the concept was included in the BRAIN model as a way to break the cycle of stress/frustration, shift from the brainstem to the neocortex, and change the chemical makeup of one's body. In Part Two (which began with the clarity of our highest purpose and our past), this third step is designed to give us a concrete method of ensuring that we are in the most productive part of our brain and are clear about where we want to focus our energy before we engage those "challenging" situations and/or people that in the past have been problematic. This step can also remind us of the value of shifting up into this higher-order thinking if we find ourselves trapped in the brainstem.

The Serenity Prayer suggests that when armed with serenity, courage, and wisdom, we are in the best position to make the best use of our energy and efforts. Rather than continuing to rail against people and situations over which we have no control, we can accept these situations for what they are and focus our energy and attention on those aspects of life that we can influence or change.

Unfortunately, many people hold on to the belief that "acceptance" means to "give in," and thus feel defeated when they choose this way of relating to a person or situation. I believe that the exact opposite is true. From my perspective, "acceptance" in the context of the Serenity Prayer just means that we do not need some person or situation to change in order for us to respond to it on purpose. Therefore, rather than "giving in," it actually removes a block to our being influential in defining who we are regardless of the situation, and thus increases our power.

Of course, as the Serenity Prayer suggests, we must first access this state (serenity) in order to "accept the things we cannot change." Further, we must have chosen serenity and acceptance in order to have the courage to change the things we can (remember, serenity is the precursor to all acceptance, courage, and change).

This makes sense if we look at the concepts of serenity, acceptance, courage, and purposeful change in terms of how our brain works, i.e., all of these qualities emanate from the "Top of the Mind." Therefore, if we are willing to create a purposeful sense of serenity, we will then be in the appropriate part of the brain to decide where to focus our energy, i.e., whether to accept what is happening and move on, or try to change it.

In fact, we can even use the prayer and the BRAIN model to cultivate "the wisdom to know the difference." For example, we can breathe deeply 3 to 5 times saying the word "relax" on the exhale, and then ask two neocortex questions:

1. **What about this situation will it take serenity for me to accept?**

Notice the difference between this question and the more common brainstem questions we may have asked ourself in the past when dealing with challenging situations, such as: *"What is wrong with these people? Why does this always happen to me?"* Instead, asking the neocortex question, *"What about this situation will it take serenity for me to accept?"* acknowledges the importance of deciding where to focus our energy in a particular situation, and uses the neocortex concept of "serenity" as a guide.

The answer could be the fact that traffic, other people, and logistics, such as, deadlines are situations over which we have no influence. If so, this will most likely take serenity to accept, which means we must cultivate this neocortex quality first in order to deal with these situations successfully. Or, put another way, rather than continuing to beat our heads against a wall trying to change a particular person or situation, we can choose to accept "what is" and move on, which frees us to focus on the aspect(s) that we can change.

However, often change takes courage, and thus we can use the "A" in the BRAIN model to also ask:

2. **What about this situation will it take courage for me to change?**

Of course, in order to change anything, we must be able to influence it in some way, and the aspect of the situation over which we have the most influence initially is how we respond. For most people, however, it will take courage to first look inside and call upon the sort of qualities and characteristics that define us at our best before dealing with the situation at hand. Put simply, it will take courage to define ourselves first in a way that is congruent with our highest purpose before attempting to influence the world around us.

The good news, however, is that if we are able to follow the process suggested in the Serenity Prayer, i.e., cultivate a sense of serenity, accept what we can't change, summon the courage to change what we can, and then bring this more purposeful way of being to the situation, we will always be more successful. Why? Because this process ensures that we will be coming from the most intelligent, capable, flexible, and skilled part of our brain... In other words, from the "Top of our Mind."

Of course, this, like any worthwhile endeavor, is easier said than done. In fact, most people will acknowledge that maintaining this higher perspective even for a day is challenging. Life seems to keep throwing road blocks in our way in the form of stressful situations and/or people. In fact, many people would describe their day as an ever-escalating series of problematic events. They wake up in the morning, and it doesn't take long for some problem to pop up and begin the process. (See graphic below.) They put out one fire, and another seems to flare up unexpectedly which kicks their stress level up a notch. No sooner have they dealt with this problem when they are faced with yet another stressful situation, and once again their body is flooded with stress-related chemicals. By now, they are increasingly stressed, frustrated, and resentful of everything that has happened from the time they woke up, which of course limits their ability to deal with the next problem until finally, they just lose it.

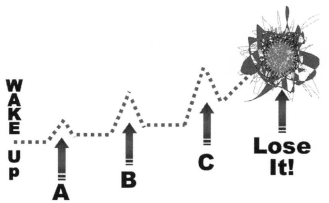

If you have ever experienced this sort of day, you know how problematic it can be, and how hard it is to change in the middle of "losing it." Most people will have to wait until that brainstorm passes before they can regain control (of course, now that you know the BRAIN model, you are not like "most people!").

It's easier to change at point "C" . . .

And even easier to change at point "B" . . .

And even easier to change at point "A" . . .

And easiest to begin before it ever starts (when we first wake up).

This means that instead of waking up and having some person or situation start us on an ever-escalating roller coaster ride to "losing it," we can ensure that our neocortex is in charge from the beginning (before we even get out of bed) by breathing deeply three to five times and saying the word "relax" on the exhale. Then we can ask the magic neocortex question: "What is my Highest Purpose? Or, what are the qualities and characteristics I want to practice (or what is the statement I want to make about who I am) this morning?"

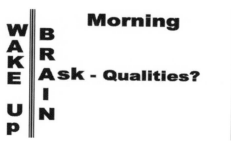

You will most likely be able to anticipate some of the more problematic situations and/or people that you will be dealing with this morning, so who do you want to be, or what are the qualities and characteristics you want to draw upon as you go into these situations? Once you have made this decision, you now know what you want to practice, and when. Therefore, you can now use your neocortex to create an image of going into the morning using the situations you encounter to make a statement about your highest purpose (who you are). Because you have created this clarity prior to the event, you are in a much better position to actually pull this off. In other words, now that you are clear about this higher purpose, you can go into the morning confidently looking to practice this process of self-definition.

Of course, this doesn't mean that nothing will bug you. Remember, this isn't about being perfect, just purposeful. Therefore, when you notice that something or someone has triggered the release of adrenaline and cortisol, you can use this as "good information," and a signal that something needs to change. Further, since you now know how to change (the BRAIN model) and what to change (which part of your brain is driving your experience), you can breathe, say the word "relax" on the exhale, and ask yourself to recall the qualities and characteristics you defined earlier. Then you can imagine yourself regaining control, and once again bringing these qualities to life and noticing the change. In fact, you may find yourself needing to use the BRAIN model to allow the "Top of your Mind" to regain control several times during the morning. But hey, isn't that better than merely surviving, or worse, allowing these situations to continue to dominate your life?

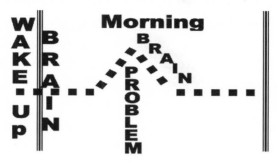

Now that you have used the morning as an opportunity for self-definition, you can (sometime around lunch) stop and look back over the experience. What did you like about what you were able to accomplish? See anything you would have done differently? Given that this isn't about perfection, and that hindsight is always 20/20, it's often valuable to use this perspective to raise our awareness of what worked and what didn't.

Okay, now it's lunchtime, and you are about to go into the afternoon. If you want to continue to use life versus life using you, this would be a great time to define what you want to practice next. Again, you will likely know the sort of situations and people you will be dealing with in the afternoon, so, what is the statement you want to make about your character?

Once this is decided, you then just go into this next part of the day using these situations to practice this self-definition. When something "bugs you," you can again use this as an opportunity to B̲reathe, R̲elax, and A̲sk the purposeful part of your brain what it wants to practice, I̲magine bringing these qualities to life, and N̲otice the change. Even if you find yourself needing to do this more than once, it will still be a wonderful way to ensure that the most clear, confident, and creative part of you is running the show.

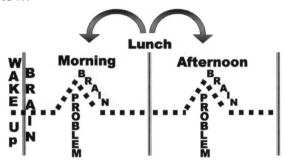

Finally, the afternoon is over, and you are either driving home or in some way transitioning between the day and the evening. This is a great time to first look back over the day and use your perfect vision (20/20 hindsight) to determine if there is anything you would have done differently. The key to success here is to see all information as "good information," and use your neocortex to imagine more purposeful responses to any situation that may not have gone as you expected.

Then, after looking back, you can look forward. Rather than just avoiding "taking work home" or moving into the evening spent and exhausted, you can instead <u>B</u>reathe, <u>R</u>elax, and <u>A</u>sk yourself, "How do I want to define myself?" and/or, "What is my Highest Purpose this evening?" or, what are the qualities and characteristics you want to practice as you go to spend time with those who you love the most and those who love you the most?

Once this question has been answered, you can then imagine bringing this higher purpose to life with those you love. Of course, this doesn't mean all will be bliss. In fact, many people report that the hardest time to "keep it all together," so to speak, is with their family. So, let's just assume that something will bug you at home. If so, you can still use life versus life using you, and take this opportunity to practice shifting from the brainstem to the neocortex by using the BRAIN model. Again, even if you have to go though this model several times over the course of the evening, you will merely be reinforcing your ability to use stress as a valuable signal, and shift to the "Top of your Mind" whenever you want.

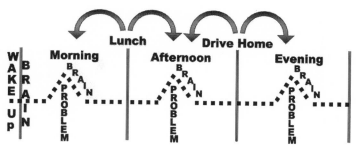

Okay, let's put this all together so that we can

see (graphically) how this information can help create and sustain a sense of purposeful serenity in our lives. As you can see in the graphic below, rather than life being a series of escalating events that result in our losing it, we can begin the day with the BRAIN Model, and return to it as often as we wish.

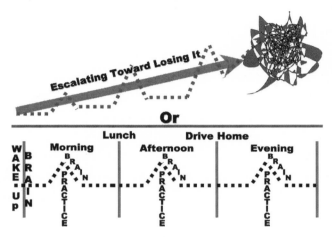

Plus, we are breaking the day into thirds, which allows us to focus on a few hours at a time and to use any situation that happens to arise (or that triggers a "rise" in stress-related chemicals) in order to practice responding in a more focused manner. Basically, we have turned the problem into part of the solution in that rather than trying to just "survive" the challenging aspects of our life, we have made them opportunities to practice shifting back to the "Top of the Mind."

The 2% Solution:

Another aspect of success here is the ability to choose a pace of action that supports our desire to bring a "Top of the Mind" perspective to all we do. Unfortunately, many people are afraid that if they don't move quickly, they will not reach their goals. We now know that this isn't the case (because we have learned that fear of anything throws us into the lower part of our brain), but it doesn't mean we won't find ourselves continuing to hurry through life trying to accomplish as much as possible in the shortest amount of time. As this quote (adapted from Sam Keen) says:

"We suffer from the illusion that the faster we run, the more likely we are to grasp happiness.
The truth is that the velocity necessary for success rarely exceeds the rate of reflection."
Adapted from Sam Keen

Therefore, in order to create the opportunity to reflect and/or think about what we are doing, and to take the edge off of the frenetic pace many of us have adopted as a way of life, I have created what I call *"the 2% solution."*

The 2% solution states that we can actually maximize our potential for accomplishment by doing everything we do 2% *slower!* The nice thing about changing our rate of activity by just 2% is that we will still accomplish what we want, and even arrive at our destinations on time. It's just that if we are willing to do all of it 2% slower, we take the edge off of the frantic nature of the experience. Plus, the decision to move at this more purposeful pace comes from our neocortex, and thus continues to support our goal of living a more purposeful life.

Of course, all of this is about bringing a sense of serenity into your thought processes, and allowing this neocortex perspective to be a precursor for everything else . . . accepting what you can't change, changing what you can, knowing the difference, and of course, using life to practice defining yourself on purpose from a "Top of the Mind" perspective.

This is why being clear about this higher purpose, our past, and the wisdom of serenity is so important. However, given that life so complex, and that I promised early on not to give you simplistic answers to these complex situations, let's move on to the last two steps, and complete the model designed to help you live "Life from the Top of the Mind."

CHAPTER 13

The Energy That Is Driving Our Thoughts, Emotions, & Behaviors

Obviously, everything that has been presented so far has to do with which part of our brain is driving our experience of life, with the goal of having the "Top of the Mind" be dominant whenever possible. In some ways, this chapter on energy is one of the most important in understanding and becoming skilled in bringing this perspective to life. However, due to the abstract nature of the concept of "energy," it is also one of the hardest to explain.

Of course, as with everything in this book, the

explanation begins with an understanding of how data is routed within our brain, the effects of this routing (which part of the brain is engaged) and the effects of the effects, meaning how all of this influences our experience of life. As we have learned, the limbic system is the gatekeeper (or the scanner, processor, and router), and when (based upon some belief or perception), this part of the brain interprets data as threatening, negative, and/or problematic, it bypasses the neocortex and sends it down to the brainstem, which immediately goes into fight-or-flight.

In some very important way, all of this is dependent on the energy that is being used to decide whether the data is threatening or benign. On one level, this energy can be described as either positive or negative. In other words, when the limbic system is interpreting data through the filters of worry, stress, anxiety, etc., the brainstem will become engaged. However, when the limbic system is interpreting the same data as "good information," or a place to practice, the neocortex will become engaged. This is easy to see when we look at the energy behind the "reactions" in the cycle of stress, and compare this with the energy behind the qualities and characteristics you have purposefully chosen to make a statement about who you are, and who you are becoming.

Another way to understand this energetic

force is to conceptualize it as either optimism or pessimism. Plus, both of the concepts of optimism and pessimism fit nicely within the models presented so far in that they represent ways of interpreting data that are based upon certain beliefs. According to the Encarta World English Dictionary, pessimism is defined as:

"A tendency to see only the negative or the worst aspects of all things and to expect only bad or unpleasant things to happen."

While optimism is defined as:

"The tendency to believe, or expect that things will turn out well" and/or "The attitude of somebody who feels positive or confident."

Can you see the basic beliefs underlying these different perspectives?

Of course, a pessimist would argue that pessimism is actually "realism," and that expecting the worst keeps them from being disappointed, and even allows them to be pleasantly surprised when something turns out well. While this may be true, I have a couple of problems with this perspective.

First, it would seem that in order to be "a realist," one must first be able to determine what is "real." On the surface, this might seem like a simple task, for all we have to do is look around us. What we can see, hear, touch, etc., is what is real and that's that. The challenge, of course, is that we only perceive a small fraction of the light and sound frequencies that exist (radio waves, spectrums of light, etc.). In other words, our five senses are not sensitive enough to hear, see, touch, taste, or smell what is really there, and thus, because we are not receiving totally complete and accurate information, we cannot rely on these senses to define reality.

I'm sure that there are some who might see this inability to determine what is "real" as a problem, however, I'm going to suggest that it's actually the good news! (Hey, I'm an optimist!). You see, one of the aspects of optimism that researchers have identified as responsible for the optimist's ability to deal with adversity and setbacks so successfully is that they are able to view the problem not so much as how things "really are," but as merely a temporary obstacle to their goal. Rather than see the situation as a failure on their part, or some confirmation of Murphy's law, optimists simply step back, reevaluate their options, and move on with the belief that they will eventually succeed. This means that their thoughts are on ways to succeed (neocortex) versus frustration and/or worry about the problem (brainstem), and because what we focus on expands, what is expanding are their options and strategies for success.

The second problem I have with the philosophy of "expect the worst and therefore you will never be disappointed" is that I wonder if the result is really worth the price? In other words, given that we now know the role beliefs, interpretations, and expectations play in creating our emotions, behaviors, and overall experience of life, if we are continually expecting the worst, our limbic system will always be "on guard," and thus will keep sending data down to the brainstem. This will, of course, limit our ability to respond to either fight-or-flight, which may not be the best way to deal with the situation at hand.

Plus, we now know that any image we hold in our mind changes the chemical makeup of our body (whether it's actually happening or not!). Therefore, given that any "expectation" is generally experienced as an image of what we expect to happen next, when that image is negative (i..e. when we expect the worst), we will be continually flooding our body with adrenaline and cortisol, which not only traps us in the brainstem, but also undermines our health, success, and well being.

If you remember earlier in Chapter Ten, "Clarity About Our Past," I told you of a psychologist by the name of Martin Seligman, Ph.D., and his research on the concept of "Learned Helplessness." Interestingly enough, he is also one of the world's leading authorities on motivation, and has done quite a bit of research on optimism and pessimism. These studies suggest that optimists are more successful than pessimists in almost ever facet of life... in personal relationships, and even in college. According to Seligman, the reason for this success is because optimists persevere and are more creative in the face of adversity than pessimists. Plus, they have better physical health and may even live longer.

All of this makes sense given what we have learned about how positive and negative beliefs affect which part of our brain is engaged, and the type of chemicals that are released as a result. Further, it seems that this tendency to interpret data in an optimistic versus pessimistic way is not innate, but learned. This explains why Dr. Seligman calls his bestselling book on the subject, "Learned Optimism."

This is good news for those of us wanting to have more influence in our lives because if this is about how we have learned to interpret data in the past, we can now become more purposeful in this process of interpretation, and choose to see incoming data in a way that engages the most capable part of our brain. In fact, we can learn to do this even when (or maybe especially when) the data seems to be less than positive. Or, put another way:

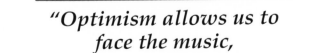

"Optimism allows us to face the music, even when we don't like the tune."

In other words, even when optimists are

not particularly happy with the "tune," or what is happening at the moment, they are able to "face the music" in such a way that allows them to change the channel or even rewrite the score. If this ability appeals to you, I suggest that we compose the music of our lives from a perspective that envisions the eventual success of both the composer and the composition.

Of course, even the most optimistic people experience stress and frustration from time to time, so let's see if we can view what some would describe as negative energy from a positive perspective, or at least see it as "good information" or a valuable awareness. To do this, I want to offer a quote that came to me while working with a client. It says:

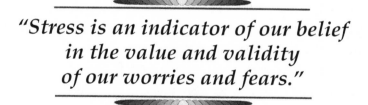

"Stress is an indicator of our belief in the value and validity of our worries and fears."

While some may view this as a statement about the problem, seen from a "Top of the Mind" perspective, it shows how even stress can be used to support a more purposeful way of being. For example, it states that stress is actually an indicator. Remember earlier in the book when I spoke of stress as a valuable signal..."Stress is a signal that something needs to change"? This is what I mean when

I describe stress as an indicator of something. It is an indicator that we may be holding on to a certain kind of belief (or interpretation) that is being driven by the energy of worry and fear. In other words, to the degree we invest our worries and fears with value and validity (which means see them as both true and valuable, or helpful), we will experience negative stress. However, rather than making this just one more thing to worry about, we can see this stress as "good information," as an indicator that we are holding on to beliefs, interpretations, and expectations that do not serve us.

This brings a new level of awareness to the experience of stress (remember Dr. Einstein's wisdom, "Problems cannot be solved at the same level of awareness that created them"). From this new perspective, we can now understand how the energies of worry and fear engage a very specific part of our brain and change the chemical makeup of our body. Given that this is often incongruent with what we want, we can change the energy we are using to drive/create our state of mind. In fact, we can even use the BRAIN model to facilitate this change by first breathing deeply, saying the word "relax" on the exhale, and then asking the neocortex question, "What is the energy I want to choose to drive my experience of life at this moment . . . positive or negative, optimism or pessimism, worry or awareness?" If we choose to be positive, optimistic, aware, etc., then we can begin to practice using these energies to influence which part of our brain is engaged and to define who we are.

Unfortunately, some people have trouble with this more positive perspective, especially as it applies to people. They may feel that they have been open and trusting in the past, expecting the best from everyone, and that they have been let down, or even betrayed in some way as a result. Further, they may believe that if they let go of this sense of betrayal (i.e. forgive and forget), that it might happen again. Therefore, they hang on to the image of what happened and the pain it caused in order to keep themselves safe.

In my presentations, I generally illustrate this point by choosing someone from the audience and asking the group to imagine that I've been in a relationship with, or working with this person, and they betrayed and/or offended me in some way. At this point, I will walk up to the participant and ask him or her to stand. As they do, I will pick up their chair as a representation of the pain that they "caused me," and drape it over my shoulder, because, hey! I don't want them to think that it was "no big deal," and I certainly don't want them to think that they got away with it, or that they could do this to me again. I've got to protect myself somehow. So, I'm going to carry this grudge (their chair) as a symbol of what they did to me, and a reminder that I should never let this happen again.

Now I am looking for somebody very different from that last person to connect with so that I won't be let down like I was before. At this point (still carrying the chair), I will walk up to another person and speak of how nice they are and how I'm convinced that they won't hurt me, but guess what? They do! Here I ask them to stand and again take their chair as a representation of the pain that they caused, and as a reminder to not let this happen to me again. I continue this with two or three more people until I have chairs (my "protective" pain), draped all over me.

I then turn to the audience and ask, "Who wants to be in a personal or professional relationship with me now?" The point I'm wanting to make, of course, is that nobody can even get close to me because of all the pain/grudges I am carrying around. Further, rather than protecting me, what the pain is really doing is sapping my strength (it takes a lot of energy to continue to carry all this pain), as well as keeping me stuck in my brainstem and separate from my higher-order thinking.

How important do you want that person to be in your life?

Another reason for getting good at letting go of the past is that doing so serves to minimize the importance of negative people and events in our lives. You see, when we are holding on to images of what was done to us, we are (without meaning to) making that person the most important thing in our life, because we are giving them the power to trigger stress-related chemicals and throw us into our brainstem.

We don't want them to have this sort of power, and therefore we must be willing to choose something more important... say, our peace of mind, the ability to regain control from our past, so that we can move into the future with clarity, confidence, and creativity. Your choice.

Of course, the goal here is to introduce the energy of forgiveness as helpful and even necessary to living life from the "Top of the Mind." And therefore, rather than seeing forgiveness as an energy that will set me up to be disappointed again, or a perspective that "let's them off the hook," I suggest we use it as a statement of self-definition.

That's why I love the quote that states:

"Forgiveness is the realization that you are no longer harmed."
Or
"Forgiveness is the decision that I will no longer hold on to painful images of the past to protect myself in the future."

The truth is that forgiveness, or our "forgiving" another (or even ourselves) has nothing to do with letting anyone off the hook. What it's really about is making a purposeful choice about whether we are going to use the pain of the problem (and a vision of ourselves as harmed by that pain) as a way to protect ourselves in the future. If this seems incongruent with your vision of life, you might consider letting go of that pain and creating a vision of yourself as "no longer harmed."

So, now we can add forgiveness, or letting go of the past to the energies of awareness and optimism as examples of drivers that should support your decision to approach life from the "Top of the Mind."

There is one more concept I'm going to suggest before we move on to the final step of this second model. This suggestion is specifically for those of you who would define yourselves as perfectionists. First, let me say that I understand and admire the drive of a perfectionist. These are generally people who are very conscientious and have a deep desire to do and be their best. In fact, they may believe that if you are not going for perfection, it means that you just don't care, and these people care quite a bit.

The problem with expecting perfection from yourself and others, of course, is that "perfect" is rarely (if ever) achieved, and thus you are setting yourself and everyone else up for failure. So, what energy can we choose that is both achievable and ensures that we will bring our best to life? I suggest the energy of excellence, especially as it is defined in this quote from Ronnie Max Oldham:

Excellence is the result of:
Caring more than others
think is wise,
Risking more than others
think is safe,
Dreaming more than others
think is practical, &
Expecting more than others
think is possible.
Ronnie Max Oldham

I see this as an "excellent" quote and perspective for several reasons. First, there is a clear message here that who we are and how we approach success cannot be based upon what others think. In other words, while some people might tell us not to care, risk, dream, or expect too much from ourselves or others, we don't have to follow their advice. In fact, according to Mr. Oldham, it is our willingness to reject these limitations and care, risk, dream, and expect more than others that will determine the degree to which excellence is the driving energy in our lives.

Second, when we go for excellence versus perfection, we not only set an attainable goal, we don't limit where we can go after the goal is reached. With perfection, once it is attained, there's no way to improve. You can't become "more perfect." With excellence, however, we can always become more excellent and increase our ability to care, risk, and dream more than before. Therefore, since success is always about continual improvement, I am recommending excellence along with awareness, forgiveness, and optimism as choices for what energy drives our thoughts, feelings, and decisions.

Bottom Line: Don't use the Energy of the Problem to Create the Solution!

The important thing here is to choose a neocortex energy if you want to live life from the

"Top of the Mind." While this statement would seem to be common sense, unfortunately it isn't common practice. In fact, most people do exactly the opposite. They become stressed and frustrated, and then they attempt to use this energy to solve the problem. This means that they run the problem over and over in their heads until their worries or concerns motivate them to take some action.

We now know why this rarely works. The experiences of stress and frustration are first generated by the brainstem. These negative emotions then re-engage this lower 20%, thus limiting our ability to access the most intelligent, capable part of our brain. As stated earlier, the energy of the problem cannot/will not create a solution, and thus, we always want to first choose an energy that is more congruent with our highest purpose, or what we want (versus what we are afraid of) as a creative force.

As promised, here is a way to use the BRAIN model to choose and install such an energy. We can ensure that our neocortex is in charge by going through the first two steps (breathing deeply and saying the word "relax" on the exhale), and then we can ask the neocortex question:

"What is the energy I choose to drive/influence my thoughts, emotions, and behavior in this situation?"

Or, we can use the Four Criteria to evaluate and, if necessary, change the energy that is driving our life. For example, we can ask:

1. Was this energy chosen on purpose?
2. Is it working for me?
3. Is it helping me make the statement I want to make about who I am?
4. Would I recommend or teach this energy to someone I love?

If the answer is "No," then we can choose an energy that would meet these criteria: i.e. that is chosen on purpose, that does help us create the experience of life we want, that does make the statement we want to make about who we are and finally, that we would recommend to those we love. We can then imagine bringing this energy (awareness, confidence, excellence, love, forgiveness, etc.) to life and notice the change, or become clear about how this way of being might be different from how we might have dealt with this situation in the past.

Of course, you don't have to limit yourself to the energies I have suggested. You can choose anything you want. You must, however, choose an energy deliberately, or "on purpose" because otherwise these choices will be made for you by your habitual beliefs formed in your past.

CHAPTER 14

The True Meaning of Responsibility

I f you remember, we are talking about the value of the C^3 lifestyle, or how increased clarity, confidence, & creativity will help us live "Life from the Top of the Mind." So far, we have discovered the importance of coming from a specific part of our brain, and being clear about:

• Our highest purpose,
• Our past (i.e., our habits and preconceptions)
• The wisdom of serenity, and
• The energy that is driving our thoughts, emotions, and behavior.

To complete the model and give us all of the tools we need to bring more confidence and creativity to everything we do, we must also become clear about the role "responsibility" plays in our lives. While this would seem to be obvious (who doesn't think that people should be more responsible?), have you noticed that the act of "taking responsibility" is becoming a lost art? Cries of "Not my job," and/or "I'm not responsible" seem to be much more prevalent today than, "I take full responsibility for this."

Why do you think this is? If the quality of responsibility is so universally admired, why do fewer and fewer people want to claim this as a defining characteristic? I believe the reason behind this refusal is that many people see the act of taking responsibility as dangerous. They are afraid that if they take responsibility and something goes wrong, then they will be to blame. As we have learned, any time we perceive anything as dangerous, our limbic system sends that data to the lower 20% of our brain, and thus, we will interpret our taking responsibility as a potential threat.

Given our recent understanding of what is happening here, I suggest that we draw upon what we have learned in step two of this model (Our Past) and change the belief that is causing this response (which will, of course, change the response). In other words, if our old interpretation/belief around the concept of "taking responsibility" isn't serving us, I suggest we replace that belief with one that is congruent with the statement we want to make about who we are, and who we are becoming. I suggest that we make responsibility less about, "Who's to blame" and more about our "ability to respond"

Response-ability...
Our Ability to Respond

Further, if our goal is to be able to respond to life in a way that is congruent with our highest purpose (the qualities and characteristics we identified earlier), then I suggest that we take 100% responsibility for our ability to respond!

To be clear, this doesn't mean that we should now become responsible for everyone else. Taking 100% responsibility for our ability to respond simply means that we are not going to wait for some situation or person to change before we decide who we want to be in response.

In fact, drawing from the material presented in Chapter Nine (Clarity of Purpose), we are moving beyond simply "not needing something to change." We are actually using the situation to practice defining who we are. Of course, as mentioned earlier, this is easier said than done. However, if our goal is to become more influential in every aspect of our lives, and operate from the Top of the Mind," this will only be possible if we are taking 100% responsibility for how we respond to the challenging aspects of life, versus blaming other situations and/or people for what we think, feel, and do.

For those of you who have found the BRAIN model helpful in accessing your neocortex and making the most of each step in this second model, we can continue that process here. For example, as you have done with the four earlier steps, you can breathe deeply, say the word, "relax" on the exhale, and ask the magic neocortex question:

"If I were taking 100% responsibility for my ability to respond to _____ (whatever situation you happen to be dealing with at the moment), *what would that response look like? How would I be thinking, feeling, and acting differently?"*

Then, you could imagine responding to life in this new, more "able" manner, which not only has your body changing chemically as if the experience were real, but also gives you a clear vision of what you want to practice. You then can notice the change you have produced in yourself, and go into life noticing the changes in who you are, and how this more purposeful, "Top of the Mind" way of being effects everything you do.

As mentioned earlier, I like the models that I create to spell something meaningful so that they are easier to remember, and also reinforce the material introduced. Therefore, this second model spells

POWER (**P**urpose, **O**ur **P**ast, **W**isdom of Serenity, **E**nergy, and **R**esponsibility) because it is designed to help us become more influential and / or powerful in our lives, and to some degree, the lives of others.

Further, as we combine the POWER model with the **C³** model, we can begin to see how each model supports the next.

For example, in terms of *clarity*:

• When we become clear about our highest purpose, (or the statement we want to make about who we are) and bring this sense of clarity to every situation (especially those that in the past we would have defined as difficult or challenging), we become more powerful.

• When we become clear about our past, meaning the old habits, learned reactions, and our "piece of the P.I.E." or our perceptions, interpretations, and expectations that are incongruent with this higher purpose, we can change the beliefs that are driving us to ones that support the statement we want to make about who we are, and we become more powerful.

• When we become clear about the wisdom of serenity, or the value of using serenity as a precursor to accepting what we can't change so that we have the courage to change those aspects of our lives over which we have the most influence, we become more powerful.

• When we become clear about the type of energy we want to drive this process, and actively choose this energy to motivate our thoughts, emotions, and behavior, we become more powerful.

• And finally, when we are willing to take 100% responsibility for our ability to respond so that we need nothing to change in order to practice this "Top of the Mind" perspective, we become more powerful.

Clarity Creates Confidence:

With this clarity of purpose, our past, the wisdom of serenity, energy, and the importance of responsibility, we are able to go into any situation with confidence because we will know why we are there and what we want to accomplish (i.e. using life versus life using us to make a statement about who we are).

Without this clarity, however, we will just continue to react to life as we have in the past. Of course, this too can be "good information," for when we find ourselves caught in this old cycle, we can excuse ourselves and use the BRAIN model to break the cycle by shifting from the brainstem to the neocortex and changing the chemical makeup of our body. We can then become clear about our purpose, our past, the wisdom (importance) of serenity, the energy we want to use, and our willingness to take responsibility for it all, and this will allow us to re-enter the situation with the confidence of a "Top of the Mind" perspective.

Clarity & Confidence Allow Creativity:

Of course, this isn't to say that just being clear and confident will always result in success. Life is almost always more complicated than we expect, and thus we will need to be very creative in how we approach each situation. The good news is that this creativity (which is, of course, a "Top of the Mind" neocortex quality as well) will be much more accessible when we begin with the sort of clarity and confidence I have described, and when we continue to remain in the upper 80% of our brain.

The best way to do this is to ensure that the data we receive is continually sent up to the neocortex rather than down to the brainstem, and the best way to do that is to interpret this data "oh purpose," almost as if it is being filtered through our clarity, confidence, and creativity. Again, this is the "good information" versus the "ain't it awful?" perspective which allows us to see the incoming data in terms of awareness versus worry. This ensures that the data is sent up to the neocortex and then recycled through the limbic system which actually trains the limbic system to interpret life in this way.

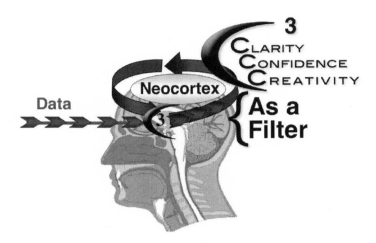

The reason I point this out is that some people are concerned that this "Top of the Mind" perspective is just about being "intellectual," as if there is no emotional component in the model. While this is understandable, it couldn't be further from the truth. I believe that emotions are a vital part of life, especially the sort of fulfilling, meaningful life that I have been alluding to in this book.

In fact, as a person who attempts to practice what he preaches, in my work as a psychologist and public speaker (as well as my other roles as a father, husband, and friend) I bring a LOT of emotion to who I am and what I do. It is the quality of our emotional experience (and how this experience affects the quality of our lives), however, that should, in my humble opinion, be chosen "on purpose."

Okay, now we know what the problem has been and what we can do about it. We have learned how to see situations such as deadlines, meetings, and traffic as opportunities to practice living "life from the top of the mind," and have been given several models to support this process. Let's move on to see how all of this information can be applied to what many have said is the most challenging of situations... dealing with difficult people.

However, before we go there, let me make one suggestion. You might want to stop reading for a short while (a week or two should suffice), and practice applying what you have learned to some of the more "static" triggers, such as deadlines, red tape, traffic, etc., before attempting to use this philosophy with the difficult people in your life.

One reason for this suggestion is that it is easier to practice defining oneself on purpose and to engage the "Top of our Mind" when there is only ONE brainstem involved. Difficult people bring their own beliefs, preconceptions, worries, and concerns to the encounter, and this extra brainstem energy can make dealing with these individuals extra challenging.

It would most likely serve you, therefore, to first become skilled at changing the chemical makeup of your body and shifting to the "Top of the Mind" in situations that don't directly involve other people before moving on.

Plus, as you practice this way of life, it gets easier and easier. Just as learning any new skill (a new language, a musical instrument, a new piece of software) can be difficult at first, the more you practice, the easier this becomes because you are actually rewiring your brain by creating new neural pathways that go from the limbic system up to the neocortex versus down to the brainstem.

The key is to have the dedication and determination to keep practicing even though this way of life may seem unfamiliar at first. Therefore, I suggest you begin each morning by asking the neocortex question, "what is my highest purpose this morning" (just the morning) and go into life with the goal of defining yourself in a way that you would teach or recommend to someone you love... reboot (using the BRAIN model) around lunch time, and go into the afternoon clear about who you are and what you want to practice... and reboot on the drive home so that you go into the evening with this clarity of purpose.

Soon, this way of life will become your "second nature," or how you automatically show up in life, and you won't have to practice so deliberately. However, for a short while (two months or so), making this a daily practice will be required to rewire your brain. Then you can begin learning how to deal with difficult people, or those resistant others who, in the past, have seemed so problematic.

Part III

CHAPTER 15

Dealing with People "On Purpose"

I am going to frame this material on becoming more influential with others in terms of some of the more challenging or difficult individuals that we encounter, because most everyone tells me that it is these "difficult" people that in the past have triggered the most negative reactions. In other words, even when we had a disagreement with someone, if they were willing to sit down with us and discuss the situation, it didn't necessarily turn into a problem. However, when "the other" responded by being defensive, angry, argumentative, or even just resistant to our point of view, often this resulted in a negative reaction on our part as well.

As you might imagine, the way the "Top of the Mind" philosophy conceptualizes the problem of difficult people is congruent with its conceptualization of problems in general. External stimuli (in this case, difficult people) have been perceived by our limbic system as threatening, dangerous, and/or problematic in some way, which has resulted in the lower part of our brain becoming engaged, and certain chemicals being released in our body. Or put simply, in the past when we were dealing with people who were argumentative, stubborn, defensive, angry, arrogant, etc., we tended to respond in kind, i.e. we became defensive, resentful, insistent, and even angry and stubborn as well.

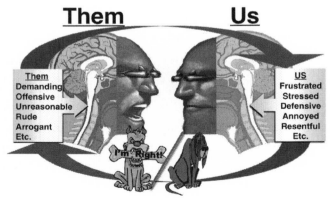

This created the now familiar cycle (in this case, the cycle of conflict/resistance) which resulted in our becoming trapped in the brainstem.

While similar to the cycle of stress, unfortunately, the cycle of conflict/resistance creates unique and often more problematic results. In other words, when we find ourselves becoming frustrated with situations, such as, traffic or deadlines, the problem is generally limited to ourselves and our experience (traffic only seems to get worse rather than actually reacting to our reaction.) Difficult people, on the other hand, will almost always react to our reaction and actually become more difficult because they are trapped in their brainstem. This negative reaction shuts down communication, and often disintegrates into an argument about who's right, who's to blame, and who needs to change.

Further, the ramifications of this negative interaction are rarely limited to the moment. The energy behind this interaction can stick with us throughout the day or even the week, and color our mood and/or mind in such a way that limits our ability to access our best thinking. Plus, this sort of encounter can also color how we interact with the difficult individual in the days and weeks ahead. Rather than creating a future environment of cooperation, or even starting our interactions with this person with a blank slate, we instead begin with one foot stuck in the brainstem.

In addition, because they have labeled us as the difficult person, they are often motivated to go and tell someone else about the incident. This "someone" could be another person on our team or in our family, their best friend in the organization, our supervisor, or anyone they think will agree with them, or is in the position to make us pay for "how we treated them."

Of course, this rendition (which generally begins with, "You would not believe what so-and-so just said/did to me!!") is from their point of view, and thus we come off looking like some irrational deviant that is obviously wrong. Now we have the added problem of having to deal with the fallout from their rendition, which could include our being seen by others in the organization in a negative light, explaining to our supervisor what went wrong, or simply having to deal with the fact that we now have a "resistant relationship" with this person that will make future interactions even more difficult, not to mention the stress and frustration we are experiencing as a result of the original conflict.

Needless to say, when the "cycle of conflict/resistance" becomes our relationship with this person, something needs to change. Unfortunately, most people see the difficult person as the cause of the problem, and thus try to change "them." On one level, this makes sense because we "know" that if they would just stop being so difficult, we could reason with them and work toward a solution. The problem, of course, is that difficult people will almost always interpret any attempt to change them as criticism, and therefore react by becoming even more resistant.

In my seminars, I demonstrate this phenomena by pairing up the participants, and randomly assigning them to be either "A" or "B." I then instruct "A" to make one of their hands into a tight fist. Finally, I tell the "B's" that they have thirty seconds to get "A" to open their fist ANY WAY THEY CAN!!!!! As you might imagine, this results in a chaotic scene where the "B's" try to force their partners to open their fists while the "A's" react by increasingly tightening their grip and resisting with all their might. After thirty seconds, I stop the exercise, and determine what percentage of the group were able to get their partners to open their fist. While the numbers vary somewhat depending on the makeup of the audience, the percentage is never more than 30%, and often as low as 0%. The reason for this is that the most popular strategy used by the "B's" is the "force and pain method," which is just what it sounds like, i.e., trying to pry their partner's fist open using physical force.

I then ask all of the participants to make a fist and imagine that someone is trying to force them to open their hand, and ask them what their reaction would be. They all say that they would resist by tightening their fist or striking out at the person trying to get them to change. Of course, this is what I am wanting them to understand, i.e., when we try to force another to change, what we are actually doing is motivating them to resist us even more!

I call this the "Lesson of the Fist," and it may be one of the most important concepts to learn if maintaining a "Top of the Mind" perspective and becoming more influential with others is one of your goals.

What this means, of course, is that in order to deal with difficult people successfully, we can't try to change them first. Because they are trapped in their brainstem, they will interpret any suggestion that they should change as criticism, and as a result be come even more resistant. Or, as the "Lesson of the Fist" says:

Whenever we try to force anyone to change, they will either resist us or resent us or both, and as a result become more motivated to defend their position!

So, what can we do? Well, given that they are stuck in their brainstem, we must first ensure that we are coming from the part of our brain where we have access to our best interpersonal and problem solving skills. Otherwise, we will just be two people battling brainstems. The best way to do this is to use the feeling of "stress" (frustration, anger, annoyance, etc.) as a valuable signal that we are coming from our brainstem and use the BRAIN model to shift to the neocortex or "Top of the Mind." This means becoming very aware of how we are reacting to difficult people, and being willing to stop the interaction and make this shift before we attempt to solve the problem.

The challenge is to do this (stop the interaction) in such a way that they don't feel as if their issue(s) are being dismissed or "blown off." In a meeting, this can be accomplished by just excusing yourself to go to the bathroom, or to "check some data in your office." Here you can practice the BRAIN model, and return having engaged the most clear, confident, and creative part of your mind.

If the interaction is more extemporaneous, or less formal, you might accomplish this same end by saying something like, "*I really want to understand your perspective on this issue. Unfortunately, at the moment I have another appointment waiting, and thus can't give your situation the attention it deserves. Let's plan to meet* (sometime within the next 24 to 48 hours), *and I will be in a better position to focus on your concerns."* Now they can see your wanting to postpone the meeting as valuable to them because you will be more open to the information they want you to know. (Later I will show you why this information is so valuable to you as well, and how to use it to become more influential in the interaction.)

Okay, we now know that if we try to force others to change (or even suggest that they are wrong), this will only drive them deeper into their brainstem and motivate them to "tighten their grip" and resist us even more (the Lesson of the Fist). In addition, we know that in order to be successful with these resistant individuals, we must have shifted from our brainstem up into our neocortex so that we have access to our best thinking and our clarity, confidence, and creativity.

Finally, we also know that we don't want to be continually falling back into the brainstem and having to shift up into the neocortex, but instead, we want to find a way to come from this upper 80% consistently, especially when dealing with difficult people and situations. Therefore, the next section explores how the models presented earlier support this consistent "Top of the Mind" perspective and, additionally, how to motivate others to shift to the most productive part of their brains and bring their best to the discussion as well.

CHAPTER 16

Difficult People & Our Highest Purpose

A s in Chapter Nine, "Clarity about our Purpose," this first step is designed to ensure that (a) we have chosen our response deliberately or "on purpose," (b) that this response is congruent with the statement we want to make about who we are, (c) that these choices are being made by our neocortex versus our brainstem, and (d) that these choices are also congruent with the effect we want to have on the interaction.

Notice that I positioned "the effect we want to have on the interaction/other person" last on the list. Why? Because this is often the first and only thing people want to accomplish when dealing with others. They want to either prove them wrong, or at minimum, change them in some way, (i.e. make them stop being so difficult!).

While this is understandable, we now know that even if we are "right" and/or even if our desire to change them is benevolent, they (these difficult people) will very likely respond to our efforts by redoubling their opposition. Therefore, this desire to influence them must be our last consideration if we wish to be successful.

In fact, even before we explore how to be influential with people, we must first determine how important this person is in our life. In my master classes, I illustrate this concept by asking participants to imagine a difficult person that they have encountered that they don't know well (or don't know at all). This could be a driver who cut us off on the freeway, or a rude customer service agent, or even a coworker that we don't know well. I ask, "On a scale from 1 to 10 (with 10 being the most), how important do you want this person to be in your life?"

The answer I receive most often is "0," which certainly makes sense. However, if we define "important" as who we allow to change the chemical makeup of our body, there are two ways to make someone important. We can love them and that makes them important. Or, we can resent them or be angry with them, and that also makes them important.

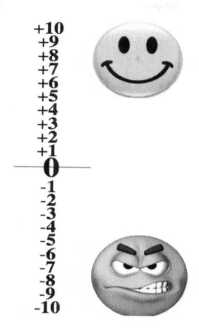

+10
+9
+8
+7
+6
+5
+4
+3
+2
+1
0
-1
-2
-3
-4
-5
-6
-7
-8
-9
-10

In other words, when we get upset at bad drivers, rude service people, or others that we don't know or at least don't know well, *we have made them the most important person in our life!*

What's the alternative? Well, if we truly want them to be a "0" or minimal in terms of importance, we need to become clear about how we relate to people who have little to no importance in our lives. Chances are this means we might notice their behavior, but we don't take it to heart, or make it something we get upset over. In fact, we probably don't give it a second thought.

On the other hand, if the person is someone

we will be interacting with in the future, then this makes them a bit more important. And, given how our careers can be affected by how people see us (whether they want to work with us, recommend us to others, etc.) then we may want to be as influential in these relationships as possible without having them dominate our thinking.

And, of course, if this is a good friend, a family member, or someone we are in a relationship with, then obviously this person is very important. The value of making this determination is that we now have some idea of the time and energy we want to put into influencing this relationship. Dealing effectively with others (especially those who are upset with us or resistant to what we are saying) takes a lot of skill and energy, and if we try to become influential with every difficult person we encounter, we quickly become exhausted.

Okay, let's assume we have decided that the person in question is indeed important enough for us to spend our time and energy on. I do plan to give you a model for becoming more influential with these people. However, we will not be able to use this model successfully until we have shifted to the "Top of our Mind," chosen our response from this upper 80% of our brain, and made practicing this response our highest purpose, or the most important thing we are doing.

In order to make this process powerful and

relevant to your life, I suggest you once again get a clear picture of the situation, i.e., first make a list of the types of difficult people you have found to be most troublesome. Then, across from each, note the quality and/or characteristic you want to practice when you next encounter one of these people.

Feel free to consult the list you made in Chapter Nine, for you may find that some of the qualities you defined there are also ones you would choose in the sort of specific situations we are describing here. However, don't feel you must limit yourself to these qualities, because you may also discover that there are some very specific qualities that you want to practice with specific types of difficult people.

For example, you might decide that when dealing with people who are stubborn, you might want to practice *patience* or *curiosity*. Or, when dealing with people who, in the past, have triggered feelings of intimidation, you might want to practice *confidence*.

There is, of course, no wrong answer here. The only requirements are that this list be made, and that the qualities chosen be positive versus "less negative" (unafraid, less angry, less intimidated, etc.) because, as we have learned, until we have a clear, positive, vision of who we want to be, what we want to practice, and/or the statement we want to make about ourselves in these situations, we will remain at the mercy of our old habits and brainstem reactions.

Now that we have defined what we want to practice, the challenge is to imagine using these encounters to bring these qualities to life. This can take place first in our mind, which means that it is very likely that we will be successful because we are controlling all aspects of the situation with our imagination. This isn't a problem unless we imagine the difficult people changing so that we feel better. We may not want them to be that powerful in our lives, and, even if they are important, we don't want our ability to choose our response to be dependent on them changing. Or, put another way,

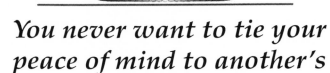

You never want to tie your peace of mind to another's state of mind.

Therefore, for the moment, just imagine them being as difficult as they want while we are practicing our chosen response.

This is similar to the imaginary island and the "difficult individual" I spoke of in Chapter Nine where we discussed hiring an actor to play their part while we practiced responding "on purpose," and decided to just use the "real life" difficult person for free!

Basically, the idea is to create an imaginary scenario where the environment was created specifically for us to practice. The value of this exercise is that (a) we have drawn information about who we want to be from the "Top of our Mind" versus just talking about being less reactive, (b) rather than worrying about them and thus making them the problem, we are making them part of the solution by using their behavior as an opportunity to practice, and (c) this process gives us a chance to create this image first in our mind where we have the ultimate influence. This is important because the first step in accomplishing anything, especially anything as intense as dealing purposefully with difficult people, is to first be able to imagine ourselves doing it successfully.

Of course, as you might imagine, actually being able to respond this way in "real life" is quite another matter, and that's why this is only the first step in the POWER model as it applies to dealing with people. Further, I promised an additional model that will help you become more influential with these difficult people by actually motivating them to shift from their brainstem up into their neocortex.

The problem, as I have mentioned, is that many people want to do this first (changing the other) and now we know why this will never work. In fact, in order to put ourselves in a position to be influential with others, we must do much more than just imagine it happening, so let's continue on and discover how the POWER model supports us in this process.

CHAPTER 17

Difficult People, Our Past, and Our P.I.E.

A s we have learned, we don't come to these encounters as blank slates, but instead, we bring a whole host of learned beliefs, habitual responses, Perceptions, Interpretations, and Expectations to the experience. In addition, the difficult person also brings their own learned perspective or "piece of the P.I.E." to the encounter, and this is one of the reasons why interactions such as these can be so volatile. Therefore, if we want to be able to influence our emotions, behavior, and experience with these individuals, as well as have some influence over their emotions, behavior, and experience, we must be very clear what creates these aspects of life. As we learned in Chapter Ten, it is not just the "fact" that someone is upset with us that causes us to react in old, defensive, and / or offensive ways, but our belief about what this means (interpretations) and our expectations about how it will effect our lives.

Therefore, in order to be successful in situations such as these, we must first ensure that we truly understand this creative process, and have chosen how we want to use this model to support our goals. Let's begin with "them." In other words, if their difficult emotions and behaviors are being driven by certain beliefs about themselves and the world, I suggest that we seek to understand these "drivers" so that we can begin to use them versus them using us. (Remember, understanding doesn't necessarily mean agreement.)

If we look below the surface of a difficult person's behavior, we will first see that he/she is stuck in their brainstem, and therefore we must assume that the limbic system has engaged this part of the brain because it interpreted certain data (maybe us) as threatening. Further, because we now know that their interpretations are created by their beliefs and perceptions, we must also assume that this person has certain beliefs about us, himself/herself, and/or the world that is causing all of this to happen.

For example, would you imagine that this difficult person sees the world as safe or unsafe? Also, what do you suppose this person believes about the concepts of trust and cooperation? Further, given the reactive quality of his/her emotions and behaviors, what would you imagine this person thinks of themselves...high self-esteem or low?

When answering these questions about a difficult person, it's easy to see how they might see the world as unsafe (i.e. people are out to get them) and further, how these people would tend to reject the qualities of trust and cooperation as dangerous.

The trick is to not be fooled by their arrogance, or what seems to be "confidence" in the righteousness of their position. This is not a sign of high self-esteem, but of low. When someone is truly confident in who they are and what they believe, they have no need to attack others. In fact, it is because of their confidence that they can become curious about an opposing position without feeling threatened.

"True confidence is the ability to listen to almost anyone or anything without losing your temper or your perspective."

It is actually the person who is afraid that there is something wrong with them (low self esteem) that needs to dominate others and/or prove others wrong. Thus, when someone is being argumentative, defensive, arrogant, etc., it is a clear sign of a lack of self-confidence and/or low self-esteem.

Why is this important to us? Because, when we are dealing with someone who believes that the world is a dangerous place, that trust and cooperation are dangerous, and that there is something wrong with them, and we respond in old, reactive ways (i.e., we become defensive, annoyed, and argumentative), we become part of the problem. In other words, when we respond to their brainstem from our brainstem, without meaning to, our reactions will reinforce their fear-based beliefs about themselves and the world, and thus support the very behavior we want them to change!

This is why dealing with difficult people can be so...well...difficult! As we have learned, they see us as the problem, we see them as the problem, and as a result, the cycle of conflict/resistance is born and exacerbated. We now know that we can't start by trying to change them because they will only interpret this as criticism, which means that we must start by changing our beliefs about them if we want to be successful.

This, of course, is easier said than done because when someone is being arrogant, argumentative, and generally obnoxious, it's easy to see them as unacceptable, offensive, reprehensible, and just plain wrong! However, now we know that if we hold on to this belief and/or interpretation, we will not only validate their negative beliefs about us, but also engage our brainstem and limit our ability to respond in a purposeful manner.

Therefore, let's examine how we might choose to see or define these people in a way that engages the "top of our mind" instead.

Basically, this means being willing to define "them" on purpose, or in a way that is both accurate <u>and</u> allows us to choose our reaction. Given that people who are being stubborn, defensive, argumentative, etc. must be coming from the part of their brain designed to deal with fear (their brainstem), then it would follow that we could accurately describe them as "frightened."

"Those that love to be feared and fear to be loved, they themselves are more frightened than anyone."
Saint Frances de Sales

Maybe not frightened in the traditional sense of someone recoiling out of fear, but more in terms of how we could describe the energy behind their behavior. As we look back at past interactions with difficult people, we could probably put, "They were worried or afraid that ..." in front of what they were thinking. For example, they were afraid that we thought they were wrong... we wouldn't listen...we didn't understand the seriousness of the situation... we wouldn't give them what they want, etc.

In fact, before learning about what is really going on here (how people become trapped in the brainstem), we could have also defined ourselves as coming from the worried or fear-based part of our brain as well. In other words, we were afraid that they would make us upset, they couldn't be reasoned with, they would cause more problems, make us look bad, etc.

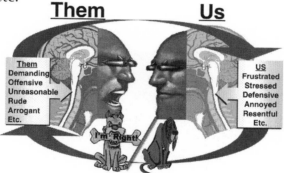

Therefore, changing how we define the problem, seeing their behavior (as well as our old reactions) as frightened versus frightening is not only more accurate, it also takes some of the threat out of how we interpret their behavior, and thus allows us to respond more purposefully.

For example, imagine that we are in a room full of friends and colleagues, and a little kid bursts in and begins telling us what horrible people we are.

We wouldn't react by beginning to defend ourselves and/or telling him that he, not us is the horrible person! No, because we would see/interpret his behavior as coming from his fear (i.e., see him as frightened), we would most likely begin to ask him questions around how we could help ("Are you lost? "Where is your Mom or Dad?" In other words, based upon our ability to see him as frightened, we are then able to respond to him from the more purposeful, compassionate part of our brain.

This is exactly what I suggest we do with what in the past we might have described as a "difficult person"... change our description of them from difficult to frightened. Not only will this diminish our tendency to see their behavior as offensive and/or dangerous, it will also give us an opportunity to respond to them in a more purposeful manner. Plus, as I have mentioned, it's simply more accurate. When we can see how another's behavior is coming from the lower 20% of their brain, it allows for the fact that this is only 20% of who they really are.

Of course, some people are so frightened so much of the time that they almost seem to live in their brainstem. However, this is not really all of who they are. It is very possible that when they are doing something they love and/or are interacting with someone they love, that they are a very different person. Why? Because in these situations, they are coming from a very different part of their brain. There is a quote I use in my presentations on leadership that speaks to this ability to see beyond the mask of resistance that many people wear when they are upset. It says:

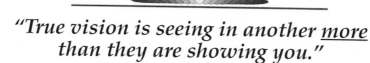

"True vision is seeing in another <u>more</u> than they are showing you."
Adapted from Neale Donald Walsch

Therefore, if becoming influential with others is your goal, then seeing their resistant behavior for what it is (the product of the frightened part of their brain) could serve you well in choosing a response. In fact, you could then become curious about who they are behind this mask, or who they are when they are not frightened, because it is this "other person" who is able to access their higher-order thinking and is the most capable of hearing what you have to say and responding intelligently. (More on how to motivate them to shift to this "Top of the Mind" persona later.)

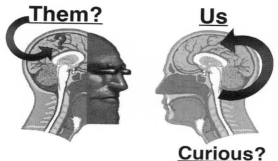

So, now we know:

- Why the cycle of conflict/resistance is so common in today's world (people are stuck in their brain stems).

- Why it is so important for us to know what we want to practice going into these situations.

- How to regain control when we lose it (the BRAIN model).

- Why these other people seem to cling to their position. (They are frightened, worried, stressed.)

- Why we must change our beliefs about them in order to be successful with them. (Because our beliefs determine how our limbic system interprets their behavior, and thus what part of our brain is engaged as a result.)

As we apply this knowledge, the good news is that something <u>will</u> change. Why? Because we have changed our part of the interaction. We are no longer doing the same "dance," so to speak.

A noted psychologist and author by the name of Harriet Lerner has written several books on this subject and interpersonal effectiveness. The perspective that Dr. Lerner uses to describe both the problem and the solution is that the way in which we respond to others and how others respond to us can be conceptualized as a dance with very predictable steps. Just as in any learned pattern of behavior, the longer these steps are practiced, the more automatic they become. From this perspective, it's easy to see how we all have been practicing certain "steps" with those we have labeled "difficult" for quite a while.

However, as we become skilled at choosing the qualities and characteristics we want to practice, as we begin to use interactions with others as an opportunity to make a statement about who we are, and as we practice seeing others who may be upset as frightened and only showing us a small part of who they really are, we can change our "steps," which then changes the dance and forces the other to change something as well.

As Dr. Lerner suggests, this doesn't necessarily mean that these "others" will always be happy about the change. In fact, they may try to force us to return to the familiar "dance" of the past because this old pattern of behavior is familiar to them, and they may fear what they don't understand. However, if we just continue to come from our more purposeful "Top of the Mind" perspective, we can weather their attempts to influence us, and do so in such a way that we actually begin to influence them. In order to do this, however, we must be applying all aspects of the POWER model, so let's continue to see how clarity about "The Wisdom of Serenity" might support us in this endeavor.

CHAPTER 18

Difficult People & The Wisdom of Serenity

Because we have already discussed the importance of *serenity* as a precursor to acceptance, courage, wisdom, and change earlier in Chapter Twelve, I won't repeat this information here. However, feel free to re-read this material as a prelude to applying this step to your interactions with others if you like, because it does pertain to what we are wanting to accomplish.

This third step in the POWER model as it applies to dealing with people, addresses our tendency to try to change "them" first as a way to resolve the conflict, and our further tendency to use our negative emotions as fuel for this change process. We now know why this won't work (the Lesson of the Fist), however, the temptation may still persist.

What the "wisdom of serenity" suggests may be the hardest thing to do in dealing with others, because it states unequivocally that in order to be successful with these people, we must first accept them as they are! I know, a part of our brain is saying, "WHAT? ACCEPT THEIR BEING RUDE, ARROGANT, DEMANDING, AND TREATING ME WITH DISRESPECT? NEVER!!!!!!!!!!

Other than noticing which part of our brain is becoming so resistant here, there is another bit of awareness that we might want to bring to the process of becoming more effective in these situations, i.e., the reason we have so much trouble with the concept of acceptance is because we see it as condoning their behavior and/or giving up, or giving in to them. To be clear, this is not my suggestion. In fact, my goal is to help you become more influential in situations such as these. However, I still say that the way to achieve this is to begin with *acceptance*.

What I mean by the term "acceptance," has nothing to do with approval or surrender, but instead is an awareness of what is, and an ability to imagine ourselves dealing with the situation without anything needing to change. It means that we recognize that they are upset, and see this less as a threat, and more as "good information" about what part of their brain is engaged, and what they believe. We don't have to agree with their rationale for being upset, but we do have to acknowledge that this is the situation with which we are faced, and that trying to change them (at least for the moment) will only make the situation worse.

The reason for this is simple. Unless we can accept "what is" (they are upset), then we will be continually trapped in the part of our brain that is threatened and needs to change something outside of ourselves before we can be effective. Given that our goal is exactly the opposite (to shift from the brainstem to more of a "Top of the Mind" perspective), we must invoke the power of serenity and acceptance because both are neocortex concepts. Remember, the "Serenity Prayer" is not a plea for serenity, but a process that describes how to use this "Top of the Mind" concept to become more powerful (influential) in our lives, and in the lives of others.

The *wisdom of serenity* with people goes like this:
1. Serenity allows us to accept them as they are (for the moment), which then allows us to focus our courage and energy for change on the area over which we have the most influence... ourselves.

2. This ensures that we are coming from the "Top of the Mind" and thus, can bring all of our clarity, confidence, and creativity to bear on becoming more influential with them.

This is also why it is so important to come into these interactions clear about the wisdom/importance of serenity, or if we miss this opportunity and find ourselves reacting from our brainstem, why it's important to use the BRAIN model to regain a sense of serenity/acceptance, and then come back to these interactions with a clear picture of what we want to practice, and who we want to be. The challenge is to recognize that the neocortex concept of serenity is the precursor for all of this, meaning that we cannot be successful with others (or with anything) unless we are able to first access this quality.

The good news is that the BRAIN model is designed to create this clear "Top of the Mind" experience of serenity. The bad news is that this has not been our habitual way of dealing with conflict in the past, and thus it will not feel familiar at first. However, as mentioned earlier, just because a way of being is unfamiliar, it doesn't mean that we shouldn't make it part of who we are. In fact, given how similar the word "familiar" is to the word, "familial," and given how many of our habitual ways of dealing with conflict were born in our family, it's very possible that our reactions to others are simply carry overs from what we learned growing up. This is not an indictment of our family, just an explanation of why some ways of being feel more familiar than others.

If you have determined that your habitual

learned ways of dealing with others are not serving you (they are not producing the results you desire and are incongruent with the statement you want to make about who you are), then these first three steps (clarity of purpose, our past/P.I.E., and the wisdom of serenity) should be very helpful in crafting new responses that if practiced will eventually feel comfortable and familiar.

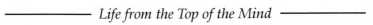

CHAPTER 19

Difficult People & Our Energy
(Getting "Them" to Shift)

When I am speaking of "energy" with respect to how we deal with difficult people and conflict, I am actually referring to two separate concepts. The first is a fairly straight forward distinction between being active or receptive, and a model for how and when to use each if our goal is to become more influential with others. The second is more abstract, but is also critical to our success, and is woven into the new model I am going to introduce in this chapter.

Yes, I am finally going to give you a model for how to motivate those "resistant" people (in the past we may have called them "difficult") to shift from their brainstem up into their neocortex so that you will (a) be dealing with a more rational being, (b) become more successful in drawing their best thinking into the problem-solving process, and (c) be interacting with the part of them that can actually hear your information as valuable versus threatening.

Of course, first we must ensure that we are applying all of the material presented to date. In other words, we must be clear about the qualities and characteristics we want to bring to the interaction, and we must have purposefully chosen our beliefs concerning those with whom we want to be influential (seeing them as frightened versus obnoxious). We also must be VERY aware of the wisdom of serenity, or the importance of accepting the fact that they are upset, not as the problem, but as good information about where to begin.

Next, we must choose whether to be active or receptive in terms of how we engage these individuals or groups. This is important because, in order for any communication to go forward in a productive way, one person must be active and the other receptive. Unfortunately, most of us have learned that the active role is the most powerful. Why? Because as children, we experienced our parents and teachers actively telling us what to do while we were supposed to be receptive and listen to their directions.

This taught us that powerful people are active and do the talking, while the less powerful (or even powerless) are supposed to be receptive, and thus we resist this "receptive" position today because it seems less influential.

However, let's look at what is going on when we are dealing with someone who is upset. Do you think this (upset) person is more likely to be active or receptive? Most would agree that these people are actively resisting what we have to say, and/or trying to convince us of something, and thus could accurately be described as being more active than receptive. So, what happens when they are active, and we respond by actively defending our position and/or trying to convince them to change? You guessed it, the "Lesson of the Fist" becomes the order of the day, and the cycle of resistance/frustration is born and exacerbated.

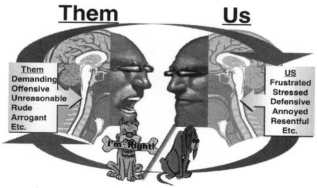

Therefore, while at some point we do want to be able to bring our ideas into the conversation and have them heard as valuable information, to do this too soon will almost guarantee failure. Even if we are being "appropriately active," i.e., presenting our views in a calm, rational manner, if they are actively resisting or defending their own perspective, they will not hear what we have to say.

Of course, this is not to say that all people are like this. There may well be many people that come to you with a problem, you take the active role and give them the answer, and they go execute your instructions. In this case, the active role is very effective because the person is being receptive to your ideas and/or directions. The problem is with those people who in the past we might have labeled as "difficult," and who we now know to be simply stuck in the lower 20% of their brain. Because these people are being actively resistant, we must begin by being receptive if our goal is to become more influential.

When I suggest a receptive position with regard to these frightened individuals, however, I am not just talking about becoming passive while they rant and rave. Neither am I suggesting that we just let them "vent" until they have "gotten it all out," and then tell them what we want them to know. Instead, I suggest that we become very curious (a receptive, neocortex quality) about what is driving their thoughts and emotions down into their brainstem so that we can eventually turn this information from the problem to part of the solution, and motivate them to shift to the upper 80% of their brain.

To accomplish this, I suggest we revisit a quote I introduced earlier in Chapter Thirteen:

"Stress is an indicator of our belief in the value and validity of our worries and fears."
Bill Crawford

It's easy to see that people who are upset are certainly "stressed" in some way. If we follow the logic of this last quote, we can see that this "stress" is an indicator that they are holding on to certain fear-based beliefs...beliefs about themselves (powerless/flawed) and the world (threatening/unsafe) that are being driven by the energies of worry and fear. (They are afraid that . . . or worried that . . .) There are several potential areas of worry and fear that could be driving their behavior, however, the overriding fear of most people who are upset is that they are going to be criticized or somehow blamed for the problem.

Part of this concern may very well stem from their awareness that indeed, they may be responsible for the problem in some way. (They didn't pay a bill on time, file a form, meet a deadline, keep an agreement, etc.) However, because this fear is tied to their self-esteem, they will be even less likely to hear your solution, especially if you forget the main rule in dealing with conflict. I call this the "You Stupid Idiot" rule, and it may be one of the most important concepts to keep in mind when dealing with people who are upset.

The "You Stupid Idiot" Rule:

You should never talk to anyone in such a way that you could end your statement with, "You stupid idiot!"

For example, with a subordinate who seems to keep making the same mistake over and over, you might be tempted to say: *"George! How many times do I have to tell you? You just can't keep screwing this up!"* (and under your breath, you say or at least think: *"You stupid idiot"*) Or, with a customer you might find yourself saying, *"I'm sorry ma'am, but this was all explained in the contract you signed last year. Didn't you read the contract?* (...you stupid idiot)." Or with anyone who is talking to you in a less than rational manner, you might be tempted to say, *"Listen, if you think you can come in here and talk to me like that and expect me to help you, you've got another 'think' coming!* (...you stupid idiot)."

I know, some of you may be thinking, "Oh my goodness, I won't be able to talk for the next three months," because when we are dealing with someone who is being arrogant, rude, and ignoring the facts, it's so easy to think of them as a stupid idiot! However, if we do, meaning if we speak to them in such a way that they can put, "You stupid idiot" on the end of our sentences, they will put it on there whether we say it or not, and thus, will respond to us in an increasingly hostile manner.

This was brought home to me very clearly by my teenage son, Christopher, who came to me not too long ago with an unusual request. He and his classmates were doing reports on what their parents did for a living, and so he came to me with this puzzled look on his face and asked, "Okay, Dad, what is it that you do again?" (You know, being a psychologist is a hard thing to describe sometimes.) I responded in what I thought was a succinct and even brilliant manner by saying, "Well, Christopher, I help people with their happiness!"

He laughed and said, "No, Dad, trust me, I can't go and tell my classmates *that*...what do you really do?" I began to describe how I give seminars and see individuals in counseling, but he interrupted and said, "No, Dad, I need a concrete example of what you actually tell people in your role as a psychologist." I said, "Okay, I tell people about the 'You Stupid Idiot' Rule." He looked at me quizzically and said, "The You Stupid Idiot Rule... what's that?" I said, "Well, I believe that whenever you are talking to someone, you should never speak to them in such a way that they could put 'you stupid idiot' on the end of the sentence." His eyes brightened, and he said, "Oh really?" and turned around and walked off. I thought, oh well, he must have gotten all the information he needed, and thus didn't give it another thought.

About two weeks later, we were having a problem with some chore he had "forgotten" to do for the umpteenth time, and I must have gone into typical parent mode, because I was saying something like, "Christopher, how many times have I told you that. . ." at which point, he interrupted me and with a little mischievous smile said: "Uh, Dad, have you forgotten the 'you stupid idiot' rule?"

Ouch! He was right. I was speaking to him in a way that he could very easily put, "you stupid idiot" on the end of my sentences. At that point, to my credit, I was able to resist the temptation to berate him even further for catching me not practicing what I preached, and instead said: "Christopher, you're right. Clearly, I'm upset right now and while this wasn't the best way to talk about it, we do have a problem here. Why don't I take a moment to calm down, and we can discuss how to solve this dilemma."

You see, if there is one thing I have learned as a

psychologist and as a parent is that up until a certain age, kids tend to define themselves through the eyes of their parents, and I would never want Christopher to think that I saw him as a "stupid idiot." However, it was true that I was speaking to him in a way that he could have easily put "you stupid idiot" on the end of my statement to him, and thus without meaning to, I was working against both of our best interests. I tell you this story to illustrate how easy it is for us to fall into this trap, and to encourage you to be very aware of how we are engaging those with whom we want to be influential, because if they sense we are being critical of them, or blaming them for the problem in any way, they will react by becoming more upset, and thus becoming more the way we don't want them to be.

To be clear, I'm not just talking about tone of voice here, I am referring to all of the nonverbals (body language, facial expression, etc.) that influence how someone interprets what we are telling them. However, rather than becoming worried and/or stressed about whether our brows are knitted or our arms are crossed in a "closed" position, all we really have to do is follow the first three steps in this model.

In other words, if we have chosen the qualities we want to practice and changed our beliefs about the person who is upset so that we see them as frightened versus difficult, and accessed the "wisdom of serenity" which allows us to accept them as they are (at least for the moment), this will go a long way toward helping us interact with them in a successful way. Or at least, in a manner that doesn't imply that we think they are a "stupid idiot."

Of course, in addition to being aware of "how" we interact with them, there is the factor of "when" to offer a solution as well. Even if we are speaking to them in a respectful way, if we try to make them let go of their beliefs, or change their position too soon, we will again only motivate them to tighten their fist and resist us even more. Therefore, given that it is clear that they are stressed and worried about something, I suggest that we begin by harnessing or working with that energy versus against it. In other words, if we can discover what is driving their resistance, we will be in a much better position to harness that driver and reverse the direction of the information.

To accomplish this, I am going to identify five of these drivers, or five ways their stress, worry, or fear might block their ability to engage in successful problem solving, and how we might effectively respond to each.

Block/Driver # 1: They are, of course, very invested in the righteousness of their position, and very motivated to convince us that they are right. Their fear is that we won't listen, and that anything we say will be an effort to convince them that they are wrong.

(This is why attempting to problem-solve or even get your point of view across at this point is fruitless, even if your solution is a good one.)

Suggestion: Listen and learn. Listen, not to placate them or "just let them vent," but to discover (learn) the key to their cooperation. In other words, what is the belief/interpretation that is driving their brainstem reaction? Holding these questions in your mind should be helpful: What are they concerned or worried about? What do they want you to know? What is most important to them as an outcome? The best way to discover these keys is to listen to what they are saying without needing to counter their logic or their position. If they are so frightened that they are not making any sense, you can ask them questions about this key, such as:

• What are you most concerned about here?
• What do you want me to know about this situation?

    And/or...

• What is most important to you here?

The important thing to remember is that you are gathering data about what is driving their brainstem reaction, not engaging in a debate about who's right. I would also suggest that you listen in a way that would allow you to paraphrase what you heard, if necessary. Of course, listening and paraphrasing are pretty standard communication tools, however,

I am suggesting that you use them in different ways than most books on conflict resolution. For example, I am not suggesting that you listen and paraphrase simply to allow the other person to feel "understood." In fact, my guess is that when most people are dealing with someone who is being arrogant and/or rude, at that moment they could care less as to whether this person feels "understood." Instead, I'm suggesting that you draw your motivation to listen from your desire to discover their driver or key, so that you can harness that energy, and at some point become more influential in the interaction.

In addition, I'm not even suggesting that you need to paraphrase everything you hear, especially if this comes in the form of just repeating what they say. For example, when someone tells you that they are feeling angry and frustrated, I am not suggesting that you then say, "I hear you are feeling angry and frustrated." Chances are they will interpret this as some technique you read in a book, and will very likely become even more angry and frustrated as a result. I am suggesting that you listen so that you could paraphrase if necessary. This is a very different form of listening than most of us practice, especially in an argument. Listening so that you could paraphrase is closer to how we listen to directions when getting to some destination as soon as possible is our priority.

For example, let's assume that we are lost on

a country road, and we are trying to get to a lake house where our friends and family are waiting on us for dinner. We stop a local and ask directions, and he says: "The old Crawford place? Sure, I know where that is. You just go on down this road until you see a big tree on your right. Then you turn left and go, say, about a mile or two until you see a pond on your left, and turn right. You then keep on going until the road goes over a big hill, and you will come to a fork in the road, and that's where you turn left. After that, you just look for a grove of trees with a house in the middle, and that's the place. You can't miss it!"

Hmmmmm... At this point, because this is very valuable information and we want to make sure we heard it correctly, we might say, "Okay, let me get this straight. You go down this road . . ." In other words, we would paraphrase what we heard to check for accuracy, because if we don't get it right, we won't be able to get to where we want to go.

This is exactly how and why we want to listen to the frightened person with whom we may be having a conversation, because what they are telling us is very valuable information about where they are, and this information will be critical to our getting where we want to go with them, i.e., motivating them to shift to the more rational part of their brain and willingly participating in the problem-solving process.

Plus, if you remember, one of their concerns is that we won't listen, and thus they may challenge us at some point by saying something like: "You haven't heard a word I have said, have you?!!" If we have been listening in this very specific way, we can say, "Well, what I have heard so far is _____. Did I get it right?" This will not only allay one of their fears (that we're not listening), it will also allow us to check to see if we interpreted what we heard accurately, which again is very important if we plan to use this information later in the discussion.

In addition, there is another reason to listen in such a way that you can paraphrase. It's very common for people who are stuck in their brainstem to go off on rants and tangents that seem to have no real connection to the original problem. They may say one or two things that are meaningful, and then go off into the wild blue yonder on some third issue that no one can do anything about. If you are listening so that you can paraphrase, this is your opportunity to interrupt them and redirect the conversation in the only way they will allow. For example, if they sense that you are wanting to interrupt them to counter their position, they will very likely resist. You can say, "But, but, but..." all day long trying to get a word in edgewise, and they will try just as hard to keep on talking, because the word, "but" signals that you are wanting to counter what they just said.

However, if you say something like, "Okay,

let me make sure I'm getting this right . . .," or even, "I don't want to forget what you said earlier. Could you tell me more about . . .," they are going to be much more willing to let you interrupt them because they are invested in you getting it right. Plus, at this point, you can paraphrase what you heard them say on the first two pertinent points (leaving out the tangent), and ask them to tell you more about these issues. You will be amazed at how this refocuses the conversation on the more germane information, and moves the process along at the same time.

Block/Driver # 2: They are afraid that we don't get it, that we don't understand the seriousness of the problem, or that we believe they shouldn't be (or have no valid reason to be) so upset. They not only believe that their problem is a "serious" one, they believe that they have a "right" to be upset about it. In fact, they may even interpret your not being upset as you don't think their problem is a big deal, or that you just don't care.

For example, if you have ever tried to tell someone who is upset to just calm down, they generally don't say, "What a wonderful idea. I never thought of that. Thank you for sharing." In fact, they will probably say something like, "Calm down? Don't tell me to calm down!," and become even more upset.

Remember the "Lesson of the Fist" which

says: *"Whenever we try to force someone to change, they will either resist us or resent us, or both, and as a result, become more motivated to defend their position!"* In this situation, our trying to calm them down could very well be interpreted as an attempt to change them, or to imply that they are wrong, which, of course, will only motivate them to defend their emotions and the righteousness of their position. So, what can we do? How can we respond in a way that allows them to stop defending the seriousness of their problem, and their right to be upset?

Suggestion: Empathize: I know, this can sound like psychobabble, so let me explain. By "empathize," I don't mean that you need to "feel their pain," hold their hand, or become their counselor. In fact, this step, while essential, takes only a few seconds, and could be accomplished as easily as saying something like, "I can see how you would be upset by this." Many people have trouble with this concept because they are afraid that in order to empathize with someone's position (or why they might be upset), they must agree with them. The important thing to remember here is that;

Understanding doesn't necessarily mean agreement!

It just means that given what we now know

about how negative beliefs can drive someone into their brainstem, we can see how they might be upset. For example, imagine you are dealing with a person who is angry because he believes that he has been treated unfairly in some way. If you were to say, "I don't know where you are getting this. You are being treated just like everyone else!," he would most likely become even more angry, and redouble his efforts to defend his position. If, on the other hand, you said something like, "I can see how you would be upset by that," it wouldn't mean that you agreed with him. It would, however, allow him to give up the need to defend his position or his right to believe what he believes, and thus he would be more open to what you have to say next. This leads us to the third block to effective communication, and yet another driver of their brainstem reaction.

Block/Driver # 3: They are afraid that we either don't value their opinion, or that we are going to continue to argue for the fact that we are right and they are wrong. This concern is understandable because, in the past, I'm sure that most of the people with whom they have disagreed have indeed argued with them about who's right. However, this is also where we can become more influential in that we are not going to respond like "most people." In fact, now that we have information about what is important to them (gathered in Step One: Listen/learn), and have used Step Two (empathize) to defuse their need to defend their position, we can now begin to encourage them then to shift from their brainstem up into their neocortex.

Suggestion: Ask A Neocortex Question. In the same way we shifted from our brainstem to our neocortex by asking neocortex questions, such as, "is this the way we want to be defined?" or "would we recommend this way of being to someone we love?," we get them to shift by asking neocortex questions versus brainstem questions.

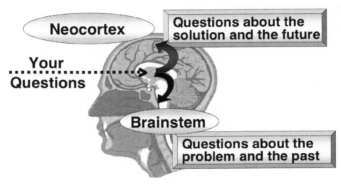

Brainstem questions are generally about the past and the problem, and are heard by most people as an attempt to identify "who's wrong." They can include, but are not limited to: Why did you do that? What do you expect me to do about it? Where did you get that idea? What were you thinking? How many times do I have to tell you . . .? etc. These types of questions will also almost always violate the "You Stupid Idiot rule," meaning that one could easily put "You Stupid Idiot" on the end of the phrase, and thus increases the likelihood that the person you are attempting to influence will be driven further into their brainstem, and become even more resistant.

Given that the brainstem is not where you want them to be, I suggest that you instead ask "neocortex questions," which are questions about the future and the solution. These will differ slightly depending on the type of conflict you are dealing with. For example, if you are dealing with a customer, this could be as simple as asking, "What is your vision of a solution here?" or "How do you see this being resolved so that it is fair to all concerned?"

Unfortunately, many people are afraid to ask these sorts of questions because they are worried that the person will ask for something they can't deliver. However, I suggest that even if this is the case, asking this question is a very important step because it moves the focus of the discussion from the past and "who's to blame," to a discussion about the future and a solution. Almost every discussion involving conflict is about *who* did *what* in the past. Unfortunately, this will be a fruitless debate, because they will remember it one way while you will remember it another, and both of you will be trying to prove the other wrong. Therefore, one benefit of asking a question about what they want in the future is that at least we are now discussing what will *be*, versus what *was*, and the discussion is no longer about "who's to blame."

The second reason for asking the, "What do you see as a solution?" question is that it gives you even more information about what is important to them, and thus more information about the key to their cooperation. Often, people (especially customers) seem to think that in order to get anyone to pay attention to them, they must be upset (the "squeaky wheel" syndrome). Therefore, they may act very upset when what they are wanting is actually no big deal. By asking, we know exactly what we are dealing with, and might find that we can accommodate them much easier than we first thought.

However, even if they demand "the moon," so to speak (i.e. ask for more than you can deliver), I still say that asking them is a good idea because it puts us in a position to know what to do next. For example, once we hear what they want, we might say, "Okay, I will need to check with my supervisor to see what we can do. Can I call you (name a specific time in the immediate future), and let you know what I found out?" If we ask this question, they will very likely allow us that time, and it might prevent them from demanding to speak to our supervisor right now and in the future.

Of course, if we do this, we must follow through on our promise to check it out, even if we know (or think we know) that what they are asking for is impossible. The reason for this is (a) if we are a person of integrity (highest purpose), this is what we told them we would do, and thus it's about keeping our word, (b) in checking it out, we may be surprised to find that what they are wanting (or at least something close to it actually is something that can be done, or (c) if it can't be done, we will want some suggestions on what we can do to help this person. That way, if we must go back to them and let them know we can't do what they asked, we can follow this up with, "However, I did discover some things that *can* be done." Often, if a customer truly believes that we have tried to accommodate their wishes by checking the situation out with others, they will be more willing to modify their original demands, and listen to what can be done.

On the other hand, if the person with whom you are dealing is a peer or family member (or anyone else whom you have known for a while), and they are accusing you of something you didn't do, you can apply the neocortex concept here as well. After first listening (without defending yourself), you can move directly to asking a "top of the mind" question, such as, "Hmmmmm, is this really congruent with (does this really fit with) who you know me to be?" Most people will be caught off guard by the question, which is good because it means that this has interrupted their brainstem thinking, and thus created an opportunity for them to shift up to the "top of their mind." This will also have them thinking twice about accusing you unjustly in the future because they know they will be asked this question.

Of course, if they respond to the question, "Is this congruent with who you know me to be?" with "Yes, it is!," then a second neocortex question might be in order, such as, "Really? What have you seen me do that would give you the impression I am that kind of person?" This should have them reassessing their criteria for accusing you, and again should affect whether they continue to do this in the future. What is important, however, is to note that in none of these cases did we defend ourselves, or match their brainstem energy with our own.

If you are dealing with a supervisee, or someone over whom you have some authority, you will want to approach the conversation differently. Usually in these situations, the supervisee has made some mistake, and you are wanting them to correct the situation and avoid this sort of problematic behavior in the future. Unfortunately, most people try to accomplish this by focusing on the mistake and the problems it caused. While this is understandable, this tact is rarely successful because this emphasis on the pain of the problem will only drive the supervisee deeper into their brainstem, and thus limit their ability to bring their best thinking to the learning process.

Given that our goal is to ensure that they shift

to the "top of their mind," we can begin by listening to their side of the story without the need to either agree or argue. This will take a lot of skill and patience, however, it is a critical component of success because (a) they are probably afraid that we won't listen, and (b) by listening, we can learn what they are concerned about, and/or what is important to them (the key to their cooperation).

Even if what we hear is some story about how they are not to blame, this can become very important information because it gives us a place to start. In other words,

In order to influence someone, we must start where they are!

Or, put another way . . .

If our goal is to motivate others, we must begin with what is motivating them!

This means that our starting point must be the part of their brain and the belief, interpretation, or concern that is driving their emotions and behavior. When someone is becoming defensive about who's to blame, this indicates that they are stuck in their brainstem, and are being driven by their desire to avoid being seen in a negative light. This is good information because it allows us to partner with this desire (empathize), and ask a question about the future versus trying to force them to admit to and/or feel bad about what they have done in the past.

In other words, rather than argue with them about whether they are to blame, we can empathize with their desire to be seen in a positive light (a neocortex concept) by following their declaration of innocence with, "Yes, I can see how you would be upset by this. In fact, it sounds like it's important to you to be seen as a valuable member of this organization."

As you might imagine, few people would argue with this statement, and thus we now have switched the discussion to the importance of success in the future versus avoidance of blame. Given that their success is something we want as well, we can follow their agreement with something like, "Good. I've got some ideas about how I can help you with this. Ready to move forward?"

Again, few people will answer "No" to this question, and thus the conversation can now be focused on what was learned, and their ability to influence how they are perceived by the organization. Once they have agreed to your helping them succeed, you can continue in this vein and have them reexamine their mistake by saying something like, "Okay, let me make sure I'm not telling you something you already know. Given that your goal is to be seen in a more positive light, and knowing what you know now, how would you do this differently in the future?"

This question has them rethinking their behavior from more of a "Top of the Mind" perspective versus "who's to blame." If they have trouble coming up with a response, you can give them another way of looking at the problem by asking, "If you were teaching someone to do this in a way that would have the most potential for success, what would you suggest that they do?"

As you can see, listening, empathizing and asking neocortex questions are critical steps in dealing with people when they are upset. What you may or may not have noticed, however, is that all of these steps are receptive in nature. This is what I mean when I say that when dealing with conflict, it is the receptive position that is initially the most powerful.

Plus, these steps change the color of the interaction in a way that makes the last step, problem- solving, more successful. In other words, our willingness to practice these receptive skills will not only give us valuable information about the key to their cooperation and allow them to shift from their brainstem to their neocortex, it will gradually reduce the "us versus them" nature of the conflict, and allow them to see us less as an adversary, and more as an ally.

Of course, at some point, we are going to want to take an active position if our goal is to be influential with this person. I just want to caution against going to the active step of problem-solving too soon, i.e., before you know the key to their cooperation, and/or before they have shifted from the brainstem to the neocortex.

How will you know if it's too soon? They will balk at your solution. This could come in the form of a "Yes, but . . .," or "I tried that and it didn't work," or some other statement that lets us know that the real key to their cooperation, or what's really important to them, is missing in the solution we offered. If this happens, the challenge will be to see this response as "good information" (versus a problem that will engage our brainstem), and repeat steps 1-3 to determine what we missed.

Of course, in the best case scenario, when we ask a neocortex question, they will give us a solution we can support, and we just go with it. I say "best case" because when the solution comes from them, it will automatically contain the key to their cooperation, and thus they will be much more likely to support its implementation. At this point, the problem-solving stage is simply about confirming logistics and moving forward with a mutually agreed upon plan of action.

What is more likely, however, is that we will need to bring all that we learned from the first three steps into the problem-solving stage and blend this information (what's important to them and what's important to us) in a very purposeful manner. This might sound something like, "Okay, I know that you are wanting (fill in the blank with what you learned in step one and three), and I am wanting (insert what is important to you). Based upon what you said, I think that there is a solution that will work for both of us. I suggest (insert your "blended" solution here). Would you be willing to give this a try?"

There are several important components of this problem-solving statement that are worth noting:

1. It begins with our conceptualization of what's important to them. This not only assures them that we heard them correctly, it gives them reason to be optimistic that at least some of this is being incorporated into the solution.

2. It states what is important to us. Interestingly enough, if this is done correctly (in the right way and at the right time), this can be a reassuring factor versus a problem. Why? Because they are more likely to trust someone who is up-front about what they want versus someone who either beats around the bush and/or attempts to hide their agenda under pleasant psychobabble.

3. The solution isn't framed as a "take it or leave it" proposition, but instead as something that is worth

trying. This is almost always the best way to suggest a solution because it helps the person(s) we are wanting to influence feel more comfortable with the idea, because they know that if it doesn't work, there will be an opportunity to revisit the decision. People will almost always be more willing to "try" something rather than be forced to either accept or reject a proposal out of hand.

Of course, before you even move to the problem-solving phase of this process, you must decide whether this is the best time to offer a solution. Often, people are so invested in their position and trapped in their brainstem (angry, frustrated, etc.) that they are not open to hearing any feedback as valuable. Therefore, postponing the problem-solving phase of the discussion often has the effect of allowing them to calm down and think about the questions you have asked. In addition, it can also give you time to think about how you are going to frame the solution, or how you are going to blend their key with yours.

The good news is that you have listened to them and learned what is important to them and what they are concerned about (the key to their cooperation). You have empathized with them so that they no longer need to defend their right to be upset, and you have asked them neocortex questions about their ideas, which gives them the opportunity to shift to the "Top of their Mind" as they think about the future and what they want to accomplish, versus the past and who's to blame. If you have determined that postponing the discussion and giving everyone time to think about the solution is the best idea, the challenge will be to do so in a way that they will hear it as good information. This might sound something like, "Okay, you've given me a lot to think about here, and I can see how important this is to you. Plus, I believe that this deserves my best thoughts. Therefore, I suggest we get back together (be sure to name a specific time in the near future), so that I have a chance to think about all of this and come up with a solution that works for everyone."

One final tip... remember to use the magic word "and" versus "but" as a transition from the receptive position to the active. Many people have learned that it's a good idea to acknowledge what another says before they offer their own opinion. Unfortunately, when this is done using the word "but" as the transition, it will likely fail, because "but" negates whatever comes before it.

For example, imagine during a disagreement someone says this to you, "Yes, I hear what you're saying, BUT . . ." Chances are that you will not be eager to hear what comes next because your position was negated with the word "but." It's like going up to a member of your organization and saying, "Sally, you have really been doing a great job, BUT . . ." The words "you are doing a great job" are immediately negated by the word "but," and thus the person with whom you are wanting to communicate will not be inclined to appreciate what you have to say next.

Instead, use the word "and." For example, "I hear what you are saying AND I have some ideas about the situation as well." This allows people to be more open to what you are about to say because you have not negated what they just said. In fact, you have set up a situation where you can draw from what they think/believe/want, and what is important to you in crafting a solution. This increases the potential that your solution will be heard in a positive light because you have included something that's important to them.

This is especially true when you are in a position of leadership or authority, and are wanting to correct someone's behavior. In fact, thinking of "correcting" this person's behavior in terms of, "How can my solution be valuable in helping them get what they want?" is an excellent way to conceptualize how you might want to frame your suggestion for change. Or, put another way:

The most effective form of correction is when the other feels informed versus chastised.

As you may have noticed, this most recent model which is designed to help resistant individuals shift from their brainstem to their neocortex spells LEAP (*Listen/Learn, Empathize, Ask* - neocortex questions, and *Problem-solve*). As I have mentioned earlier, I like my models to spell something and, whenever possible, for that word to have some meaning in terms of application. In this case, I call this the LEAP model because I believe it will take a LEAP of faith for us to practice these steps when dealing with conflict. The reason for this is that few, if any of us, grew up dealing with conflict in this way. For example, think back to when you were a child and there was a conflict in your family. How many times do you remember your parents turning to you and asking for your thoughts, and/or trying to understand your position? As before, this isn't meant as an indictment of our parents or our past, just good information on why this style of communication seems so foreign.

Therefore, I encourage you to give yourself some time to become comfortable with the process, and also to use the power of your imagination to see yourself going through the steps with people in your mind before you try it in person. In fact, starting with less intense interactions and working your way up to those individuals who have been especially problematic in the past would be a very good idea.

Of course, I do know that there are people who are so frightened that we can LEAP with them all day long and it won't make any difference. However, I suggest that even with these people, the LEAP model is the best way to respond if your goal is to maximize success. Why? Well, for one thing, the LEAP model doesn't give them anything negative to complain about. The interesting thing about "difficult people" is that if we were to ask them who are the difficult people in their lives, they would say us! They see our reaction as the problem, and even use this reaction to justify continuing, or even intensifying their original resistant behavior. When we are able to react by listening/learning, empathizing, asking, and then problem-solving (remembering the "You Stupid Idiot!" rule), we don't give them any "ammunition" to fire back at us or complain about. What are they going to say... "They just listened to me too much?," or "They were too interested in what I had to say?"

In my work as an organizational consultant and speaker, I have had the pleasure of interacting with a wide variety of people and organizations. While good customer service/communication is becoming increasingly important to all of my corporate clients, one group in particular has highlighted the importance of following a model, such as LEAP in their dealings with people who are upset. That group is the 9-1-1 dispatchers and telecommunicators who answer the phones twenty-four hours a day, all across the nation.

Just imagine, you are answering a 9-1-1 emergency call, and the caller is being rude, obnoxious, arrogant, ... your typical "difficult person." In this case, however, communication (the ability to get information from them, and have them listen to what you have to say) isn't just a good idea, it could be a matter of life or death. Plus, every word you are saying is being recorded . . . and might wind up on the evening news!

Think of the last time you found yourself in conflict with someone who was upset, and imagine another person was standing there with a video camera getting the whole thing on tape! This will give you some idea of the degree to which this group of under-paid and under-appreciated public servants need a purposeful and professional way of responding. They must interact with every caller in a way that not only maximizes the potential that they will get the cooperation they need, but also allows them to maintain a professional demeanor, regardless of how abusive the caller is being. In my work with these public servants, they have told me that the LEAP model is valuable because it gives them a way to stay engaged with the caller without falling either into the cycle of conflict or the brainstem, and even allows them to maintain a professional perspective that they would be proud to hear on the evening news.

So, even if the person we are dealing with refuses to cooperate no matter how much we listen, empathize, etc., the fact that we have responded purposefully and professionally can serve us in that we have kept our cool, and acted in a manner that if someone were observing our interaction, we would be seen as a professional. Plus, our ability to choose our response and define who we are regardless of the situation reinforces the fact that no one has the power to make us feel bad or force us to react in a negative way, even if they resist our attempts to influence the interaction.

In fact, for those of you who have taken the time to list the qualities and characteristics you want to practice when dealing with resistant individuals or groups, you should find that the LEAP model is very congruent with this vision. For example, if "professional, patient, confident, and flexible" are representative of the "Top of the Mind" qualities you have chosen as how you want to define yourself, the willingness to first *listen* with genuine curiosity, *empathize, ask* neocortex questions, and then *problem-solve* is a behavioral model designed to bring those qualities to life.

Put another way, this is how professional, patient, confident, and flexible people interact with the world. Thus, like the BRAIN model, the LEAP model should be helpful to those of you wanting a more tangible, concrete way to make these qualities a part of your self-definition.

Speaking of the BRAIN model, for those of you who have found this behavioral model helpful, you can certainly apply it to dealing with resistant individuals as well. For example, when we are willing to take the time to breathe, rid ourselves of tension, and ask ourselves neocortex questions (such as, how do I want to define myself at this moment?) and then imagine ourselves being this way with these people, we will also be in the best position to motivate them to shift to the "Top of their Mind" so that we can all move into productive problem-solving in a more "purposeful" way. This may be challenging in the "heat of the moment," however, so do remember that there will be times when we just need to disengage from a particularly intense interaction, and go somewhere and use the BRAIN model to change the chemical makeup of our body, as well as shift to the "Top of our Mind." Once we have accomplished this, we will then be in an excellent position to go back into the interaction and proceed in a way that has a much higher potential for success.

Okay, so far we have discussed the cycle of conflict, or how simple disagreements can escalate into a self-perpetuating cycle, and we have learned that when we attempt to solve the problem by trying to change "the other" first, they become even more resistant (the Lesson of the Fist).

We also have discovered how their beliefs about themselves, the world, and us (as well as our beliefs about them) can have a powerful effect on their behavior and on our ability to solve the problem. Further, we have examined the many reasons (stress, worry, fear) why people may be resistant in the first place, and learned a model (LEAP) that not only deals with each reason, but increases the likelihood that they will hear our suggestions in a more favorable light.

Of course, we can always use "The Four Criteria" to increase our awareness of how we want to interact with others. For example, we can ask ourselves, if we were dealing with this person:

1. On purpose or deliberately . . .

2. In a way that works for us or has the effect we wanted . . .

3. In a way that makes a purposeful statement about who we are . . .

And finally,

4. In a way that we would teach to a child... what would this look like?

Regardless of how we do it, all of this flows from dealing with people with an awareness of our higher purpose, as well as making a decision to first employ the receptive energies of curiosity and empathy, and then shifting to the active energy of purposeful engagement/problem-solving.

Rather than trying to change them, we are instead tying what they want with what we want, and then creating concrete agreements that bring out the best in them and support the best for all concerned.

Recently, I have expanded this model to include two blocks or obstacles to effective communication and influence (prior to the LEAP Model), and an antidote to each. The first is, of course, our state of mind. As we have been discussing, when we are stressed, frustrated, annoyed or even simply tired and drained, we will not be in the "Top of the Mind," and as a result, will not have access to the sort of interpersonal skills and problem-solving skills that are necessary to deal with difficult people.

Plus, this stress and/or annoyance will very likely creep into our tone of voice, and the person we are talking to will very likely put "you stupid idiot" on the end of what we say, which will, of course, prevent them from wanting to hear more.

The antidote to this is being very clear about our highest purpose, or the qualities and characteristics we want to bring to this interaction. And, we need to be willing to bring these to life, *regardless of how they are being* (remember, we don't want to tie our piece of mind to their state of mind).

The second block or obstacle to effective communication and influence is our trying to stop their negative behavior, for example, when we say something like, "If you would just stop being so difficult," or "If you would just listen, we could solve this problem!" As you might imagine, they will most likely here this as criticism and argue more vehemently for the very behavior you are trying to get them to change.

Instead, I suggest you focus not on what you want them to stop, but what you want them to start. In other words, you know who they are when they are coming from their brainstem. What you want to find out is who are they when they are coming from their neocortex. Have you ever seen them exhibiting the sort of qualities you are looking for? Has there ever been a time in the past when you saw them being open-minded, curious, helpful, or whatever you would like them to be with you now? If so, try to hold an image of them at their best, because that is what you want to bring out.

The LEAP Model completes the next four steps (Listen/Learn, Empathize, Ask, and Problem-solve), and puts all the information we have learned so far together to create a six step process to minimize resistance and maximize communication and cooperation.

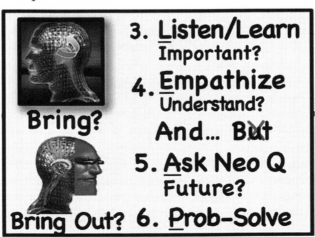

Bring?

3. **Listen/Learn**
Important?

4. **Empathize**
Understand?

And... B~~u~~t

5. **Ask Neo Q**
Future?

Bring Out? 6. **Prob-Solve**

CHAPTER 20

Difficult People & Responsibility

A s mentioned earlier, the last step in the POWER model revolves around the concept of *responsibility*, and with resistant individuals, this concept must be interpreted very purposefully in order to be successful. For example, if we define "responsibility" the way most people do (i.e., "Who's responsible?" or "Who's to blame and thus should change?"), we will be thrown into the brainstem, which will limit our ability to respond. However, if we are willing to ask more purposeful questions around this concept such as, "Who do I want in control of my ability to respond?" or, "If I were taking 100% responsibility for the quality of my responses, what would they look like?" then we can easily and effectively incorporate the concept of responsibility into our model for becoming more influential or more powerful in our lives, and in the lives of others.

In order to do this responsibly, however, we must approach our interactions with others with genuineness and sincerity. In other words, my goal in presenting these models is not to turn you into a "LEAPing robot" where you are artificially "listening," and then "empathizing" and "asking" as if you are following some script. If a resistant person (or anybody, for that matter), senses that you are using some "technique" on them, they will very likely resist you even more.

You must be genuine, which means being who you are, with your own personality and unique style of communication, versus trying to "fake" some way of interacting with people that is false or phony. I am also suggesting that you choose and emphasize the aspects of your personality that are congruent with your highest purpose. The result of this "Top of the Mind" genuineness, therefore, is you at your best, or you at your most "purposeful," which I believe also equates to you at your most "powerful."

Further, you must be sincere, meaning that you must be truly invested in reaching a solution that works for everybody. The reason I am suggesting that you must sincerely pursue a mutually-beneficial solution is that when we create outcomes where either we lose or "they" lose, I believe that everybody loses.

While lawyers might be able to argue against each other in court and then go have a drink afterwards, most people will tell you that the residue left from a win/lose encounter is counterproductive to any successful collaboration in the future. Add in the stress associated with this type of confrontation, as well as the potential that the "losing party" will go and spread negative comments about you, and you have all the rationale you need to sincerely pursue a win/win solution.

In addition to being genuine and sincere, there is another distinction we must make in order to apply the L.E.A.P. and P.O.W.E.R. models successfully. We must know the difference between "influence" and "manipulation." Often when I am presenting this material, one of the participants will ask, "Isn't this just another form of manipulation?" While I can understand the confusion, I am always just a little concerned by this question, because I know that if a participant leaves the seminar wanting to be more successful in their interpersonal interactions and yet, thinks that the information presented can be used to manipulate others, he or she will be doomed to failure.

Therefore, to ensure that I don't do you the disservice of leaving you with the impression that "influence" and "manipulation" are interchangeable, let's look at how the dictionary defines these concepts:

• *"Manipulation: to control or play upon by artful, unfair, or insidious means, especially to one's own advantage."*

• *"Influence: to affect or alter by indirect or intangible means; to act upon (as a person or a person's mind or feelings) so as to effect a response."*

Can you see the difference? The definition of "manipulation" contains the words "unfair, insidious" and "to one's own advantage," while the definition of "influence" just speaks to the concept of effecting a response. This is a good example of how the energy we choose to guide our thoughts and behavior can have such a powerful effect on the results of an interaction. Bottom line, when we are attempting to manipulate someone into doing what we want, they will sense this and resist us even more. On the other hand, if our desire is instead merely to influence, and the other can see that the outcome we are trying to create is beneficial for them as well as for us, they are more likely to cooperate.

Further, they are also more likely to see subsequent interactions with us in the same light, which increases the potential for more successful outcomes in the future. That's why I'm suggesting that the

L.E.A.P. and P.O.W.E.R. models be combined so that we are drawing upon the concepts that we believe will be the most productive and beneficial for all concerned, not just practicing some "manipulative technique."

Okay, let's summarize what we have learned so far.

• First, one of the problems in dealing with "difficult" people is that their behavior has (in the past) triggered a response on our part that not only didn't help, but actually motivated them to become even more resistant. This, of course, triggered another response in us and the cycle of conflict/resistance was born and exacerbated.

• We now know that their "difficult" behavior is being generated by their brainstem, and thus when we respond in kind, everyone is coming from the lower 20 % of their brains.

• In order for us to break the cycle and become more influential in our own lives, as well as with others, we must either start from the neocortex or use the BRAIN model to shift to the "Top of our Mind," and use the situation versus the situation using us. This means we must know the qualities and/or characteristics that we want to use to define ourselves in this situation, and be willing to practice this "higher purpose" perspective as we interact with others.

• This will only be possible when we understand

how their beliefs about us and our (old) beliefs about them are driving the negative interaction. Once we understand these drivers, we can then shift from our brainstem where we saw them as obnoxious, annoying, or even frightening (intimidating), to our neocortex where we see them instead as frightened. We are then in a position to access our curiosity, and learn what's behind their mask of resistance.

In fact, this is a good time to talk about the words we use to describe others. While seeing people as annoying, intimidating, frustrating, etc. is understandable, I suggest we choose different words. Why? Because, when gerunds or words ending in "ing" are used as adjectives, they describe another's effect on us.

When that effect is positive, or congruent with our highest purpose (inspiring, motivating, etc.), then all is well. However, given that we don't want to give others the power to annoy us, intimidate us, or frustrate us, I suggest we avoid describing them as if they can.

Now back to our review.

• Having recognized that we can't be successful with people like this by trying to change them first (You should never tie your peace of mind to another's state of mind), we can now employ the *wisdom of serenity* in order to accept that they are upset. Next, we summon the courage necessary to change what we can, which initially are the qualities we are bringing to the interaction. This means that we must initially be willing to practice our highest purpose in the face of their difficult behavior so that we can bring our best to the encounter, and begin to influence them to whatever degree is possible.

• This will require our willingness to be receptive before we become active, and listen to them in order to learn *the key to their cooperation,* or what is important to them. Once we have this valuable key, we must also empathize with them so that they no longer feel that they must convince us of their right to be upset, or believe what they believe. Remember, this doesn't necessarily mean that we agree with them.

• Once they are clear that they no longer need to convince us of the righteousness of their position, we can begin to ask them neocortex questions (questions about the future and the solution versus the problem and the past), which should give them the opportunity to shift from their resistant brain to their receptive brain.

• In order to accomplish this, however, we must be willing to make problem-solving the LAST thing we do in dealing with others, and ensure that we are bringing all we learned about the key to their cooperation to this final step. This means continuing to blend what is important to them with what is important to us until we come up with a solution that works for everyone.

• Finally, we must *take personal responsibility for our ability to respond*, regardless of how they are with us. When we are able to do these things, we will become more influential or powerful in terms of who we are and how we feel, how they see us, and finally, how they respond to us and our message.

Of course, it isn't necessary that we limit this way of interacting with others to "difficult people." The LEAP model combined with a sense of purposeful awareness (the POWER Model) is also an excellent method of communication in general. For example:

• How valuable would it be if everyone listened to each other, and fully understood what is being said before responding?

• How valuable would it be if everyone ensured that they were coming from the most productive, intelligent part of who they are in our interactions?

• What sort of misunderstandings could be avoided if everyone checked out their beliefs and assumptions before responding?

• How valuable would it be if everyone knew that everything they said and did made a statement about who they are, and thus used their interactions with others as an opportunity to define themselves in a way that they would teach to those they love?

• To what degree would you like "neocortex," or

"Top of the Mind" questions to be the energy that drives the problem-solving efforts in your group of friends?

• How valuable would it be if everyone took personal responsibility for the quality of their responses when interacting with each other?

If these questions elicit a positive response, then the next question would seem to be, "How can I bring this 'Top of the Mind' awareness and these communication skills to my interactions and / or my friends and family?" The most obvious answer is, of course, to begin practicing this way of communicating with everyone you encounter. I suggest this because "communication" always exists as a two-way street, and often the other person is reacting to us. Therefore, if we begin to practice this type of "Top of the Mind" communication, it could trigger a similar response in others.

Of course, just being a certain way with others doesn't guarantee that everyone will follow suit. Indeed, given that few of us grew up with this "Top of the Mind" perspective as a model for success, some people may be suspicious at first. They may be afraid that this is just a trick designed to manipulate them into doing our bidding, and thus approach this new perspective with caution.

This is understandable, and therefore it will be important that we continue to practice this more purposeful way of being until others see that it's not just a superficial mask, but a profound statement about what we believe to be important. This consistency, combined with the fact that a "Top of the Mind" perspective is more enjoyable to be around, will eventually either persuade them to give it a try, or let you know that, at this time in their life, they may just be too frightened to trust anything but fear as a guide for what they believe. In this case, a "Top of the Mind" perspective of compassion would be a good choice for us.

CHAPTER 21

C³ Clarity, Confidence, & Creativity with People & Life

As with the first part of the book, the LEAP model combined with the POWER model is designed to bring the **C³** or "Top of the Mind" perspective to life, especially when life is about dealing successfully with others. Therefore, when we are able to go into any situation with...

- Clarity of purpose, and being clear as to how we want to define ourselves, and/or the statement we want to make about who we are. . .

- Clarity of our past habits and how beliefs, interpretations, and expectations drive everyone's emotions and behaviors . . .

- Clarity about the wisdom of serenity, or the value of gaining this neocortex perspective before attempting to become influential with others. . .

- Clarity about the energy that we are going to use in these situations (receptive before active), curiosity, empathy, and neocortex questions before problem-solving, and finally . . .

- Clarity about the value of our taking 100% responsibility for our ability to respond so that we don't need anything or anyone around us to change in order for us to practice this higher purpose . . .

As we are able to bring this degree of clarity to our lives, we will be more powerful. One way to access this clarity is to put each of these steps in the form of a neocortex question and use the BRAIN Model to ask the question and implement the answer as the graphic below illustrates:

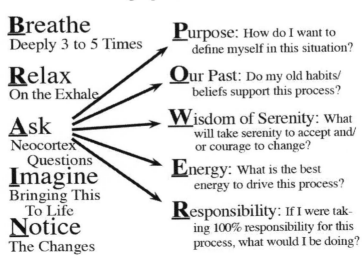

Breathe
Deeply 3 to 5 Times

Relax
On the Exhale

Ask
Neocortex
Questions

Imagine
Bringing This
To Life

Notice
The Changes

Purpose: How do I want to define myself in this situation?

Our Past: Do my old habits/ beliefs support this process?

Wisdom of Serenity: What will take serenity to accept and/ or courage to change?

Energy: What is the best energy to drive this process?

Responsibility: If I were taking 100% responsibility for this process, what would I be doing?

Then, as we become skilled at asking these purposeful questions and combining these purposeful models, we will then be able to interact more confidently with others, and access our most creative thoughts and ideas in the process. In other words, we will be able to bring our best to life, and become more influential in our lives and in the lives of others.

Part IV

CHAPTER 22

Becoming "The Cause"

A s I have mentioned, I didn't want this book to be just another oversimplification of the challenges we face, and thus I have presented several in-depth models designed to give you both an insight into the specific problems that block our ability to succeed, as well as specific solutions. That being said, however, I also want to give you ways to tie all of this together. Therefore, for those of you who would like another method for understanding and applying what has been presented, I offer this final formula:

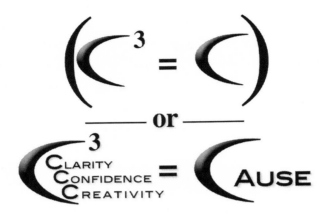

This means that when we bring our clarity, confidence, and creativity to life, we are no longer the effect . . . <u>We become the cause!</u>

If you remember, early in Chapter One, I alluded to the "Natural Law of Cycles," which states that life presents itself as a cycle of cause and effect. The problem, of course, is that when we identify the negative situations in our lives as "the cause," then we become "the effect," and therein lies the problem. We also discussed how most people attempt to solve the problem by changing this external cause. Unfortunately, because so many of the situations and people we encounter are beyond our control, this strategy almost always results in increased stress and frustration.

As I have stated, I'm not adverse to changing some external aspect of our lives if this is truly a viable option. However, for all of those times when changing a particular person or situation is more trouble than it's worth or just isn't possible, I suggest a different tact. Don't try to change the cause or even change the effect, because even if we change the effect, we are still *the effect*. Instead, become *the cause*.

This means that we first become clear about how we want to define ourselves in this situation, and then take this purposeful "Top of the Mind" way of being into whatever set of circumstances we happen to be dealing with at the moment.

The Natural Law of Cycles
Become the Cause!

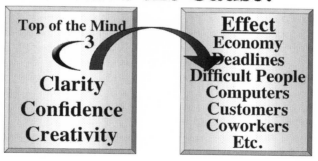

What will happen then is that the situation or the world will begin to react to us rather than the other way around. Of course, we don't know how it's going to react, and that's where the qualities of confidence and creativity come into play. However, even if this reaction is not what we wanted or expected, we can take this as good information (a neocortex perspective), and either alter our way of being or not, depending on our highest purpose.

For example, if we know we will be dealing with a person who may be upset or resistant, we can decide ahead of time what we want to practice or who we want to be in response to their resistance. This way, even if despite our best efforts to define ourselves as someone who is receptive to their concerns and open-minded in terms of a solution they remain resistant, we can still be proud of the way we participated in the exchange, and move on without allowing their fears or resistance to "make us" feel one way or another.

Again, the key is to go into the situation clear about what we want to practice. Or, if we find ourselves reacting to a person or situation in a way that is incongruent with our highest purpose, we must be willing to excuse ourselves, and reestablish our neocortex as the dominant part of our brain before we return.

Further, if you have decided that this "Top of the Mind" perspective is not just a nice idea, but a way of being that is worthy of making a way of life, then you can take the next step, which is not only becoming the cause, but making clarity, confidence, and creativity so important that it *becomes our cause,* or the most important thing we do. This means that maybe the real questions should be: what is our cause, what cause do we stand for, and/or what defines us, or what causes us to do what we do and be who we are?

As you might imagine, many people find this "Top of the Mind" concept very intriguing, and ask how long it will take to make this a way of life. Of course, the answer is "it depends." It depends on how important this is to you. It depends on how much time and energy you give it. Basically, it depends on how much you are willing to practice this way of being in everything you do. Remember, given that we are always practicing something, we will either be practicing responding to life the way we have learned to date, or making the "Top of our Mind" our highest purpose, and beginning to look for opportunities to practice bringing this more purposeful way of being into all we do.

This process of learning to move from the brainstem to the "Top of the Mind" reminds me of a poem written by a young lady going through the stages of recovery. The poem, by Portia Nelson is called *An Autobiography in Five Short Chapters,* and I offer it to you here (by permission) as an excellent example of what it means to change one's perspective on life:

An Autobiography in Five Short Chapters
by Portia Nelson

Chapter One:

I walk down the street.
    There's a deep hole in the sidewalk.
    I fall in.
    I am lost.....I am helpless;
    it isn't my fault.
It takes forever to find a way out.

Chapter Two:

I walk down the same street.
    There is a deep hole in the sidewalk.
    I pretend I don't see it.
    I fall in again.
    I can't believe I am in the same place;
    but it isn't my fault.
It still takes a long time to get out.

Chapter Three:

I walk down the same street.
    There is a deep hole in the sidewalk.
    I see it is there.
    I still fall in....it's a habit.
    My eyes are open. I know where I am.
     It is my fault. (or I take 100%
    responsibility)*
I get out immediately.

*(A "Top of the Mind" interpretation)

Chapter Four

I walk down the same street.

There is a deep hole in the sidewalk.
I walk around the hole.

Chapter Five:

I walk down a different street!

You see, what we are talking about here isn't about just avoiding the holes in life (i.e. becoming less stressed, frustrated, angry, etc.). It's about changing the way we approach life itself and making this way of dealing with life (versus life dealing with us) so powerful that it's like walking down an entirely different street!

For those of you who are wanting more information on how this can happen, or for that matter, want to know more about how any new skill is learned, I suggest that you look at a model that has been around for quite a while. No one seems to be quite sure of its source, however, it's called *The Four Stages of Learning*, and when applied to living "Life from the Top of the Mind," it can give us insight into the process of how all of this works, as well as hope for the future.

The Four Stages of Learning:

I. Unconscious Incompetence

II. Conscious Incompetence

III. Conscious Competence

IV. Unconscious Competence

I. Stage One is called "Unconscious Incompetence." This stage is characterized by a general lack of awareness. In other words, in this stage, people don't know what they are doing. Unfortunately, they don't know that they don't know, and this lack of awareness leaves them trapped in the problem, or stuck in the hole, looking for who's to blame. What generally moves them to action is that at some point the pain of the problem becomes so great that they realize something must be done.

"Most people will never change until it becomes too painful not to."

II. This leads us to Stage Two, which is called "Conscious Incompetence." While still an uncomfortable stage, at least now we know that we don't know, and for some, this can be very valuable information because it let's us know where to begin. Basically, we all must start at this stage before we can acquire any knowledge, and thus it can be seen as the beginning of freedom from ignorance.

The challenge in this part of the process is to be willing to admit that we don't know (become conscious as to why we keep falling into the same holes) and be willing to gain the knowledge necessary to move forward. Once this has happened, we can move into Stage Three, which is called "Conscious Competence."

III. Conscious Competence is where most people will be at this point of the book. We have now raised our awareness significantly. In other words, we now know what causes us to become trapped in the lower part of our brain, we know how to shift from the brainstem to the neocortex and change the chemical makeup of our bodies, and we know how to sustain this more purposeful perspective and bring it to every aspect of our lives. Basically, we know how to use life (versus life using us) to make a statement about who we are, and who we are becoming, or how to live "Life from the Top of the Mind."

However, because this knowledge is new and has yet to become a habit, it may very well take *a lot* of purposeful focus on our part to pull this off. We will have to make this new way of life the most important thing we do (our highest purpose) and think about it A LOT in order to become successful.

At this stage, we must be very gentle with ourselves because, just as if we were learning to play a new instrument, we may find ourselves hitting our share of wrong notes. However, if we are willing to keep practicing, keep looking for opportunities to choose more purposeful beliefs about ourselves and the world, and keep taking 100% responsibility for our ability to respond, we will succeed, because anything we practice over and over will eventually become a skill and a natural way of being.

For those of you who have gotten a college degree or become certified in any field of study, you have some idea of the sort of focus this requires. Basically, when getting this degree, our life revolved around the process of acquiring knowledge and becoming skilled in our chosen field of study. For several years, we paid thousands of dollars in tuition, went to classes, took notes, did homework, wrote papers, studied for tests and generally devoted a large majority of our waking moments to the successful completion of this process. For those of you who want to acquire the ability to live life from the "top of the mind" as soon as possible (say, two to six months), this is the sort of focus that will be required. That's why in Chapter Twelve, I described the process of dividing the day into three parts (morning, afternoon, and evening) with the suggestion of going into each section clear about what we want to practice.

Again, given that we are always practicing something, we will want to ensure that we are not just reinforcing old habits that no longer serve us. The way to do this, however, is not to stop the old but to start the new, and keep "starting" or practicing this new way of being until it becomes a habit. This will eventually lead us to the fourth stage of learning, "Unconscious Competence."

IV. Living in Unconscious Competence is where we feel like we are walking down a different street all of the time, because now this practiced/ purposeful way of life has become "second nature," or what we do automatically. For the most part, people in this stage interpret problems as "good information," and choose who they want to be in response, almost without thinking about it. They have become practiced at going into situations clear about their highest purpose, and therefore, even if they do become "stressed," they know that the feeling is just a chemical change in their body, and thus use this awareness as a valuable signal that lets them know which part of their brain has become engaged. Then, if they decide that the situation with which they are dealing cannot be successfully addressed from a fight- or-flight perspective, they change the chemical makeup of their body, and engage their neocortex before continuing.

In fact, given that this "Top of the Mind" perspective has become so practiced and familiar, people at this stage are able to make minute adjustments to their brain and body so quickly, that they can go into almost any situation clear and confident about who is "in charge" of their thoughts and emotions, and thus, easily access their creativity in the pursuit of what they want to accomplish. Because of this, they are often very skilled at influencing their experience of life, and even the situations and people around them. However, even if they find that despite their best efforts, things don't go the way they wanted, they are still able to access the wisdom of serenity and move on.

I say "for the most part," because as you might imagine, this process isn't about becoming perfect, just more purposeful. In other words, even at this fourth stage of learning, life will continue to give us plenty of opportunities to practice. Just as accomplished musicians never stop learning and improving, even though to those around them, they seem to be as good as one can become, so to is the "Top of the Mind" concept a process of constant learning and growth. The difference is that at this stage, the process is simply a lot more fun and thus, even when things don't go as one expects, the ability to shift one's focus and walk down a different street is so meaningful that there is little to no time wasted in the brainstem.

CHAPTER 23

Conclusion

I f you remember, we began with a quote from Albert Einstein: ***"Problems cannot be solved at the same level of awareness that created them"*** My hope is that you now have a new awareness of what is actually happening when we find ourselves reacting in old, less than purposeful ways. Rather than seeing the situations and/or people with which we are dealing as having the power to "stress us out" or "make us frustrated, angry, resentful," etc., we now know that these reactions are simply the result of data being sent to the lower 20% of our brain.

We have learned how to use this reaction as "good information" and shift up to the "Top of the Mind," and even change the chemical makeup of our bodies. Further, we have learned how to maintain this "Top of the Mind" perspective, and bring it to all we do, and even how to encourage others who may be stuck in their brainstem to make this shift as well.

There is one more quote from Dr. Einstein, however, that I would like to share with you in closing. I'm especially fond of this quote, not only for its wisdom, but because most people wouldn't expect Albert Einstein to say it. In terms of how to interpret all of the people and events one encounters, he says:

"There are only two ways to live your life, one as if nothing is a miracle & the other as if <u>everything</u> is."
Albert Einstein

One, as if all of the negative events and people in our lives "make us" feel the way we do, and the other as if these situations provide a series of miraculous opportunities for us to define ourselves "on purpose." One, as if there is no purpose or reason for all the challenges that we face on a daily basis, and the other as if purpose is all that matters. That's why I like to call this way of being, "Living and Working On Purpose," or simply, "Life from the Top of the Mind."

As I said in the beginning, this is the first time I have attempted to put everything I know into one book, and while there is a lot to remember, the good news is that the essence of each step exists in all the other steps as well. For example, if you go into a situation clear about your highest purpose, or how you want to define yourself, you will automatically be paying more attention to your beliefs, the wisdom of serenity, the energy you choose, etc. By the same token, if you are willing to take 100% responsibility for who you are and how you respond, you will also be more purposeful in terms of the energy/beliefs you choose, and what you practice. Therefore, while all of the material is designed to support you in bringing a neocortex/Top of the Mind awareness and sense of purpose to all you do, if one particular step or concept resonates with you more than another, feel free to use it to guide your choices/practice, and you should be well-served.

The key, of course, is to see your life as an opportunity to practice, and as much as possible, choose to practice "on purpose." For those of you who would like some support in this endeavor, or just wish to stay connected to the material, I invite you to go to my website (www.billcphd.com) and sign up for my free newsletter which is sent out each week, and always contains one of my favorite quotes, as well as several paragraphs about how to apply that quote to our lives. I also invite you to send me any thoughts you have about the material in this book, in that I am always looking for ways to make my ideas more helpful and easier to understand and implement.

Until then . . . Take care and God bless.

APPENDIX I

The Top of the Mind Inventory™

For those of you who like to quantify the degree to which you are coming from your most productive part of your brain, I have created a short test, or inventory that should be helpful. Keep in mind, however, that unlike most instruments of this kind, the *Top of the Mind Inventory (TMI)* does not attempt to get at what you "really think" by asking the same question in many different ways. Nor is there an attempt to keep one from skewing the results to make them "look good."

The thing to remember in taking the TMI is

that all you are going for here is awareness. No one but you will see the results, and thus, this is not the time to worry about whether or not you come out with a "good score" (a brainstem concern, by the way). As the good Dr. Einstein said, *"Problems cannot be solved at the same level of awareness that created them,"* and so I encourage you to use this instrument and your results as "good information" about what part of your brain is driving your thoughts, decisions, and emotions.

The Top of the Mind Inventory™
Created by Bill Crawford, Ph.D.

In response to the statements below, please choose one of these five responses:

Almost Always	Most of the Time	About 1/2 of the Time	Some of the Time	Almost Never
1	2	3	4	5

I tend to become frustrated, stressed, and/ or worried when...
1. I am stuck in traffic, or in a long line.

Almost Always	Most of the Time	About 1/2 of the Time	Some of the Time	Almost Never
1	2	3	4	5

2. I am faced with a deadline.

Almost Always	Most of the Time	About 1/2 of the Time	Some of the Time	Almost Never
1	2	3	4	5

3. I imagine having to give a presentation.

Almost Always	Most of the Time	About 1/2 of the Time	Some of the Time	Almost Never
1	2	3	4	5

4. I am late, or running behind schedule.

Almost Always	Most of the Time	About 1/2 of the Time	Some of the Time	Almost Never
1	2	3	4	5

5. I think about my past.

Almost Always	Most of the Time	About 1/2 of the Time	Some of the Time	Almost Never
1	2	3	4	5

6. I think about my present situation.

Almost Always	Most of the Time	About 1/2 of the Time	Some of the Time	Almost Never
1	2	3	4	5

I tend to become frustrated, stressed, and/or worried when...

7. I think about my future.

Almost Always	Most of the Time	About 1/2 of the Time	Some of the Time	Almost Never
1	2	3	4	5

8. Someone criticizes my position.

Almost Always	Most of the Time	About 1/2 of the Time	Some of the Time	Almost Never
1	2	3	4	5

9. I fail to live up to other's expectations.

Almost Always	Most of the Time	About 1/2 of the Time	Some of the Time	Almost Never
1	2	3	4	5

10. I evaluate my financial situation.

Almost Always	Most of the Time	About 1/2 of the Time	Some of the Time	Almost Never
1	2	3	4	5

11. Things don't go as planned.

Almost Always	Most of the Time	About 1/2 of the Time	Some of the Time	Almost Never
1	2	3	4	5

12. People don't do what they're supposed to.

Almost Always	Most of the Time	About 1/2 of the Time	Some of the Time	Almost Never
1	2	3	4	5

13. I make a mistake.

Almost Always	Most of the Time	About 1/2 of the Time	Some of the Time	Almost Never
1	2	3	4	5

14. I encounter one particular person, or type of person.

Almost Always	Most of the Time	About 1/2 of the Time	Some of the Time	Almost Never
1	2	3	4	5

15. I fail to reach a goal or achieve what I set out to accomplish.

Almost Always	Most of the Time	About 1/2 of the Time	Some of the Time	Almost Never
1	2	3	4	5

Now, simply determine your TMI score by adding up your responses to each of the fifteen questions.

My TMI Score _____

Now, let's plot your score on the TMI brain map.

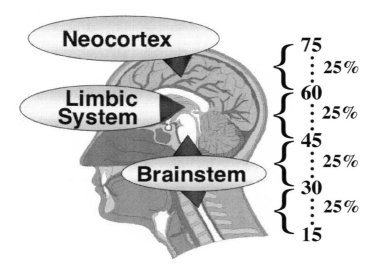

• A score in the upper 25% (60-75) means that you are coming from the "top of your mind" most of the time, and experience very little frustration, stress, or anxiety, regardless of the situation. Whatever you are doing is working well, and thus the models in this book should reinforce what you already know, and provide support for you to continue to come from this "Top of the Mind" perspective.

• A score in the 45 to 59 range means that you operate from your neocortex most of the time. However, there are also situations where stress and/or frustration may get the better of you and throw you into the lower part of your brain. Given that you are coming from the neocortex most of the time, however, you can (if you like) choose to interpret this as "good information," and apply the information in the book to the situation. Do this often enough, and you should find yourself moving into the upper 25%.

• A score in the 30 to 44 range means that you are experiencing much more frustration and stress than you like, and that you may feel unsure of what to do to fix what is wrong. This is because you are often trapped in the brainstem, and this lower part of the brain lacks the clarity, confidence, and creativity necessary to solve the problem. If you practice the models outlined in this book, however, you can begin to move up the scale and begin to increasingly engage your neocortex in the process of creating your experience of life. You might also consider engaging a professional to support you in this process so that you don't have to make this move all by yourself.

• A score in the lower 25% of the scale (15 to 29) indicates that you probably feel worried, stress, and anxious almost all the time. This is a tough place to be because neither of the two options available to you (fight-or-flight) will allow you to successfully address the problem. Plus, because you are trapped in the "undermind" so much of your life, you are likely to feel trapped and undermined by life in general, and confused as to what to do. Here is where working with the BRAIN model will be an important first step, because you must initially allow the neocortex to regain some semblance of control in order to begin to operate from this higher-order thinking. Once this is done, the material in this book should be useful in helping you maintain this perspective, and with practice, you should be able to find yourself coming from the "Top of the Mind" on a much more regular basis. Getting support from a qualified mental health professional that you trust is even more important here, because the experience of being stuck in the brainstem is so frustrating and confusing. Chances are that you wouldn't want someone you cared for having to deal with this alone, and thus you will want to ensure that you have this kind of support as well.

Of course, this inventory is not designed to be an all-encompassing, diagnostic instrument, but simply a tool to help you identify what part of your brain is dominating your thinking. As you work with the models in this book, feel free to return and retake the test, and watch your score go higher as you access your higher -order thinking.

APPENDIX II

The BRAIN Model and Sleep

In my presentations, many people describe one of the triggers in their lives as not being able to fall asleep or fall back to sleep if they wake up during the middle of the night. This is because few of us have been taught how to go to sleep, and, of course, because of our tendency to worry. For example, the way most of us "go to sleep" is just lay down and wait for it to happen. Unfortunately, when it doesn't, we begin to worry. We worry about things such as what we didn't do the day before or have to do tomorrow, etc. Soon we notice that we have been lying there "trying to go to sleep" for several hours, and we begin to worry about the fact that we will have to get up soon, and the cycle of stress is once again born and exacerbated.

Just as in other aspects of life, to break this cycle we must first understand what is happening to our body chemically in these sort of situations. If you remember earlier, I told you that stress is actually just a series of chemicals released in our body, and how these chemicals (adrenaline, noradrenaline and cortisol) can be beneficial in that they actually wake us up in the morning. The problem with going to sleep, however, is that when we are lying in bed worrying about the day before, the next day, and/or the fact that we haven't been able to fall asleep, we are actually producing wake-up chemicals! No wonder we are less than successful.

In order to achieve our desired state of restful sleep, we must first ensure that our neocortex is in control and our body is free of tension by breathing deeply three to five times, and saying the word "relax" on the exhale. Interestingly enough, this alone will begin to have us feeling more relaxed, and is a perfect prelude to sleep.

However, rather than just waiting for sleep to happen, we can speed up the process by asking the magic question: "How would I rather be feeling?" My guess is that words such as tired, sleepy, or drowsy might come to mind. Next, of course, we can imagine a time in the past when we were feeling really sleepy, when lying down and going to sleep was all we wanted to do. We further can remember how good it felt to lay down on the bed, how nice the sheets felt, etc. Then we could imagine what it would feel like right now if we were able to bring these feelings into the present. . .how nice the bed we are in feels, and how good it feels to be sleepy and tired. Finally, as we become more and more drowsy, we can imagine feeling this way in the future when just lying down begins to trigger a feeling of drowsiness and relaxation.

At this point, we will want to notice how much more sleepy and tired we are than when we started the process. Now it's just a matter of repeating the process (The BRAIN model) until we go to sleep. The reason that this works is that it focuses the brain on what you want versus what you are worried about, and because you are holding images of being sleepy in your mind, you produce "sleep" chemicals. Even if you need to go through the model several times, you will feel increasingly sleepy each time you do, and eventually you will go to sleep.

By the way, for those of you who want to become skilled at going to sleep in general, there are a few things you can do to develop this skill. First, you must be willing to go to sleep at approximately the same time each night. This will have your body expecting sleep at this time, and cooperating with you by beginning to produce "sleep chemicals" around this hour of the evening. You will also want to make sure that you do the same things each night before you go to sleep in approximately the same sequence (brushing your teeth, taking a hot bath, reading a sleep-inducing book, etc.) because this will also trigger the production of these chemicals.

By the way, when I say a "sleep-inducing book," what I mean is one that has you producing endorphins versus adrenaline. While I am a fan of certain works by Stephen King, I don't recommend reading this sort of book before you go to bed. Not only will it produce adrenaline and keep you awake, it will most likely influence your dreams so that you keep producing stress chemicals throughout the night and wake up less than rested.

Instead, I encourage you to choose all aspects leading up to sleep (the book you read, the show you watch, the person with whom you engage in conversation, and even the topic of that conversation) "on purpose." This way everything you do supports your goal of getting a good night's sleep, waking up rested, and being ready to bring your highest purpose to life.

APPENDIX III

Remembering the Face of My Father

As you may remember, earlier I mentioned that this work was a combination of material from my first two books, "All Stressed Up & Nowhere To Go!" and "From Chaos to Calm: Dealing with Difficult People Versus Them Dealing with You!" In the epilogue of the first book, I included a newspaper clipping of an article written by my father, Burton Crawford, which was published in a local east Texas newspaper sometime in the early 1950's. I have included it again here, both as a tribute to my Dad, and as a statement about how some aspects of our past can be treasures worth discovering and holding on to.

The clipping didn't have a date on it, but it had to be written sometime after 1947 because that's when Dad joined AA. Still, keep in mind that even if this was written sometime in the early 1950's, much of what we speak of today in terms of the mind-body connection, and the degree to which we create our own reality was not part of that culture. One thing this article does demonstrate is the degree to which our lives can be influenced by the environments we grow up in, and how fortunate I was to have grown up in an AA home. . .

Alcoholics Anonymous Is Force In Molding Lives.
By Burton Crawford

Editor's note: This is the last of brief daily articles written by a local member of Alcoholics Anonymous, Burton Crawford, who will speak at the Loyal Men's Bible class, at the First Christian Church, Sunday at 9:45 a.m.

One of the most important lessons we learn in Alcoholics Anonymous is that whatever comes to us in the way of happiness or unhappiness, health or sickness, abundance or lack, we attract by our own consciousness. When things go wrong the human tendency is to place the blame on circumstances or luck, but the real truth is that we have "gone wrong" somewhere in our thinking about life.

With most of us the transformation of our thoughts about ourselves and life is not an immediate but a gradual process, for the habits of years are not easy to change in the twinkling of an eye. This apparently slow process brings discouragement and the inclination to give up to many beginners in AA, for appearance rarely changes overnight. But each victory gained, however small, is a step towards the goal of a richer, happier, more satisfying life.

Each time we replace an unloving thought with a loving one we are building a consciousness of love into our life. Each time we replace a thought of fear and doubt with one of faith and confidence we are changing the pattern of our life. Each time we affirm health and abundance instead of talking sickness and lack we are becoming firmly established in the consciousness of life and richness.

A heart that is filled with love and expresses this love in kindness, consideration, and tolerance toward all attracts loving and happy experiences. A consciousness that is filled with thoughts of life and strength and vitality brings into manifestation a strong healthy body. A mind that acknowledges the everywhere presence of God establishes prosperity and order in outer affairs.

The purpose of our 24-hour program in Alcoholics Anonymous is to give us at least one constructive thought upon which to construct each day. Every time we manage to replace one negative thought with an affirmative one we make an important advance in spiritual growth. To build constructive, uplifting ideas into our consciousness is like mastering a subject by daily study. Attainment may seem far away at first, but each day's application brings its reward, and sometimes gradually, sometimes suddenly, we realize that we have achieved our goal.

The power to transform our lives lies within us. The Spirit of God is with us to uphold us and sustain us, and as we work with Him, the way is made clear and easy for us. We are assured of continual growth and life is transformed and blessed.

I have always been aware even as a small child, how important my father was to the AA community. In fact, I have many vivid memories of people relating stories of their lives and how they owe whatever success and happiness they might have achieved to him. I was always touched by their stories, and at the same time somewhat saddened because I couldn't say the same thing. That is as I have mentioned, Dad seemed to save much of his energy for those in AA, and tended to use home as a place to recharge his batteries. As I read and re-read these words, however, I am beginning to realize just how much my life has been influenced by my father's work and ideas.

I still wish he had been home more, hugged me more, not waited until he was dying to tell me he loved me, and in general, given Mom and me more of that powerful love and energy he so effortlessly gave to those in AA. Yet, as I hold the written pieces

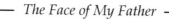

of his life, I find the compass that confirms my direction. My father, in his quest to touch others, has also left me his love. Thanks, Dad.

APPENDIX IV

Dealing With Loss And Grief

*"All connections are infused with dreams of what
is possible in the future. Thus, when we lose
something or someone important to us,
we aren't just grieving the loss, we are
grieving the shattered dream."*
~ Bill Crawford

As a psychologist and someone who has experienced loss firsthand (both of my parents died of cancer within about six months of each other when I was 21), I have come to understand that the natural, normal, healthy reaction to loss is grief.

Unfortunately, our western culture doesn't seem to see it this way. Possibly, because of this lack of vision, or because grieving can be so intensely emotional, we try to avoid it and/or describe the feelings associated with the experience of grieving in rather pejorative terms. For example, we call it "breaking down, falling to pieces, losing it, becoming a basket case," etc., and thus we find it hard to move through this process when we experience a loss.

I know that this was my experience when I lost my parents. Being a male raised in the piney woods of Northeast Texas, I thought that the way to deal with grief was to resist feeling anything, and so, when faced with the loss of my parents (and given that I was an only child in my family), I shut down and tried to feel nothing. Unfortunately, not only was I successful in this resistance, I received a lot of support for this position. People would come up to me and say "you're doing so well" and "being so strong." Little did they know that I had shut down altogether, and was just going through the motions.

Finally, after years of denial, I entered a master's program in psychology that had the wisdom to insist that the students deal with their issues before they were let loose on the public. This requirement turned out to be a blessing in disguise, because it allowed me to get in touch with these long-repressed emotions in a safe place with people that I trusted. As a result, I finally began to open up and allow myself to feel the emotions that had been buried for so long...and a very strange thing happened.

For the first time in my life, it felt really, really good to feel really, really bad.

You see, when I decided to feel no pain after the loss of my parents, I also had unwittingly shut off my connection to my love for them as well. Thus, when I was willing to open up to the pain and allow it to be a reflection of my love, I was able to give the experience of grieving a sense of purpose and meaning. The tears became a testimony to my love for the two people who had given me life.

I also noticed that I was not only grieving the loss of my parents, but also what would never be. As I mentioned, I was only 21 at the time of their death, and was just beginning to reconnect with them after my "teenage independence" phase. Not only was that reconciliation cut short, but I realized that they would never see their grandchildren, never see me earn my Ph.D., and I would never have the opportunity to give to them as they had given to me.

This "Shattered Dream" concept (developed by Chicago psychologist, Ken Moses) has come to be a major component in my work with others who have experienced a loss, and it is one I suggest you adopt on your journey from college student to adult. Whether grieving the loss of a relationship, a loved one, a job, a pet, or even just the discovery that what we thought was going to happen will never come to pass, what we are all grieving is a shattered dream. Plus, since the dream, or our vision of the future is always perfect, always about hope and what we see as possible, the resulting grief reflects the depth of this pain.

Ken Moses is the previously-mentioned Chicago psychologist who has done some excellent work in this area, not only in framing the experience of loss and grief in terms of a shattered dream, but also in understanding the value of the process itself. Here is a quote I adapted from his writing:

"Grieving is not the problem, it's part of the solution. It is an unlearned, self-sufficient process that helps us to move from the past to the future, from inaction to action...
from shattered dreams to more
purposeful dreams based upon
who we really are and
what we can create."
~ Adapted from Ken Moses

As with my other ideas and philosophies on dealing with stress, frustration, anger, etc., the first thing I feel we need to understand is how the experience of grieving is tied to the physiology of our body. For example, most people know that we have two nervous systems: the "sympathetic "and the "parasympathetic." The sympathetic nervous system is designed to gear us up to be able to fight or flee when faced with a threat or trauma of some sort. The parasympathetic nervous system is designed to bring us back to normal after facing this sort of trauma (such as loss). What many people don't know, however, is that one of the functions of this parasympathetic nervous system is the stimulation of the tear glands! Thus, crying (and the experience of grieving, in general) isn't <u>in</u> the way... it <u>is</u> the way! It's our parasympathetic nervous system kicking in to help us deal with the loss, return to "normal," and go on with life.

As mentioned earlier, this unfortunately isn't how our culture views the experience, and as a result, we are likely to find ourselves blocking the very process that is designed to help us heal and move on.

This is where Dr. Moses does an exceptional job of helping us see these emotions for the natural, normal, and even healthy "feeling states" that they are. Elizabeth Kubler-Ross was very instrumental in helping us normalize the experience of grieving early in the 1970's by describing the experience as a series of five stages (denial, anger, bargaining, depression, and acceptance). Although she did note that not everyone will go through each stage, or in this order, the fact that she defined her model as a series of stages has lead many to believe that this is what should happen. The problem with this assumption is that, as anyone who has experienced a loss knows, we don't move smoothly from one stage to another until we arrive at acceptance.

Dr. Moses, on the other hand, defines these stages as "seven feeling states of grieving," versus "five stages of grief," and I have found this alternate perspective to be very helpful. We might start with shock and denial, but then we might feel (in no particular order) confusion, anxiety, anger, fear, depression, and even guilt. Further, we can easily find ourselves re-experiencing these feeling states as they seem to wash over us much like a wave in the ocean. In fact, as with a wave, if we try to fight it, we will be unceremoniously up-ended, tossed around, and eventually thrown to the bottom. If, however, we are willing to let the wave roll over us, surrender to its natural, gravitational forces, and avoid trying to fight the experience, we can come out on the other side feeling a little lighter, and more free.

However, in order to do this, we must first see thoughts and feelings associated with grieving, not as the problem, but part of the solution . . . as our parasympathetic nervous system kicking in to help us deal with the trauma of loss. Next, we must understand why the loss affects us in this profound way… we are grieving not just the loss of a person or situation (job, relationship, etc.) we are also grieving a shattered dream. Plus, we are also very likely grieving any past shattered dreams that we resisted grieving at the time of the loss.

One way to help with this process of moving through the feeling states of grieving is to give them meaning. For example, Dr. Moses speaks of how shock and denial (generally the first of the feeling states) allow us to retreat into ourselves so that we can begin to marshall resources to deal with the loss. In other words, the reason it initially feels too overwhelming to deal with the loss is because it is actually too overwhelming! What is needed is a time of numbness so that we can create internal and external resources to help us face and accept what seems unacceptable. Anger and anxiety then move us from inaction to action, and help us begin to establish the kind of boundaries we need at times like these . . . boundaries that allow us to take care of ourselves versus always being so concerned about the needs of others that we put ourselves last on the list.

As mentioned earlier, crying can also be given a purpose. Instead of it being a sign of our failure to cope, or what we must hide to avoid making others uncomfortable, it can be a behavioral representation of our love for what or who we lost, and even a statement we make about ourselves of which we can be proud, i.e., I am a person who cares deeply, and when I lose someone or something that is important to me, I will feel sad. The alternative would be to feel nothing, which would either be a denial of what I truly felt (out of fear), or some sort of inability to feel natural, normal, healthy emotions.

When working with people who are grieving (or when grieving myself), I recommend allowing the tears to flow all the way down our cheeks and even drip onto our clothes, versus stopping them cold with a tissue at the edge of our eyes the way most people do. I encourage people to see their tears as "liquid love," or as a way to connect to and even celebrate our love for who or what we have lost. Then we can allow the wave to sweep over us, cleanse us, and even begin to wash away the pain. Anyone who has ever had a "good cry" knows this feeling. We surrender to the emotion, temporarily "losing control," and the natural, normal, healthy experience of grieving takes us to a new place... a place where the pain is not quite as bad, and yet the memory of the lost love is still as strong, or maybe even stronger because now we have learned to feel the love through the pain and give them both new meaning...a place where we move from the past to the future, from inaction to action, from shattered dreams to more purposeful dreams based upon who we really are and what we can create.

As a client I had the privilege to work with once said: "Tears are a river that takes us to places we've never been." Here's to our willingness to allow the current of that river to take us to a new place where loss is painful but not debilitating, because we have learned the art of grieving the shattered dream.

This reminds me of a quote that came to me when I was working with a client that says, "When our purpose becomes avoidance, our life becomes a void." When we are unwilling to dive into the feelings of grieving and feel them with purpose and passion, what we create is a void which leaves us void of the emotions necessary to bring our best to life.

As with everything else in this book, the key here is to engage this aspect of life with clarity about the value of the process, gain confidence in our ability to move through the process in a healthy way, and develop creativity in how we give the experience meaning and purpose. Bottom line, I suggest we take the quote I have adapted from Ken Moses to heart, and make it our mantra with respect to grief and loss: "Grieving is not the problem, it's part of the solution. It is an unlearned, self-sufficient process that helps us to move from the past to the future, from inaction to action... from shattered dreams to more purposeful dreams based upon who we really are and what we can create."

APPENDIX *IV*

Recommended Reading

If you have enjoyed this book and want to continue along this path, you might be interested in reading some of the works that have served as a foundation for much of what I know and believe. I want to take this opportunity to thank all of the authors listed below for taking the time to put their best thoughts down on paper so that others could learn and grow from their wisdom.

Bach, Richard. *Jonathan Livingston Seagull.* New York: Avon Books, 1970

Bach, Richard. *One.* New York: William Morrow & Co.,1988.

Bach, Richard. *Bridge Across Forever*. New York: William Morrow & Co., 1984.

Bach, Richard. *Illusions.* New York: Dell Publishing Co., 1977.

Bach, Richard. *Running From Safety.* New York: William Morrow & Co., 1994.

Benson, Herbert, M.D. *Timeless Healing: The Power & Biology of Belief.* New York: Scribner, 1996.

Covey, Stephen. *The 7 Habits of Highly Effective People.* New York: Simon & Schuster, 1989.

Dyer, Wayne. *Your Erroneous Zones.* New York, Funk & Wagnalls, 1976.

Frodsham, Joe. *Make it Work: Navigate Your Career Without Leaving Your Organization* Palo Alto, CA: Davies-Black Publishing, 2005.

Goleman, Daniel. *Emotional Intelligence: Why It Can Matter More Than I.Q.* New York: Bantam Books, 1995.

Ornstein, Robert. *The Roots of the Self: Unraveling the Mystery of Who We Are.* Harper Collins, New York, 1995

Seligman, Martin, Ph.D. *Learned Optimism.* New York: Simon & Schuster, Inc. , 1990.

Walsch, Neale Donald. *Conversations with God, Book 1,* New York, G.P. Putnam's Sons,1995.

About the Author

Bill Crawford, Ph.D., is a licensed psychologist, consultant, speaker, and coach based out of Houston, Texas. In addition to his keynote on, **"Life from the Top of the Mind,"** the philosophy and models contained in this book are woven throughout all of his presentations, which include such topics such as:

Clarity, Confidence, & Creativity:
New Information on the Science of Dealing
With Stress, People, & Life!

Leadership from the Top of the Mind

All Stressed Up & Nowhere To Go!

The Compass Personality System
(*Working With Different Personality Types*)

Getting Others To Get It!

To order additional copies of this book, or for information on Dr. Crawford's presentations, please visit www.billcphd.com. You may also contact him toll free at 1-888-530-8550 or reach him by email at drbill@billcphd.com.